Nelson Number Skill

3

Alan Brighous
Da

Nelson

Thomas Nelson & Sons Ltd
Nelson House
Mayfield Road
Walton-on-Thames
Surrey KT12 5PL
United Kingdom

I(T)P Thomas Nelson is an International Thomson Company
I(T)P is used under licence

First published by Thomas Nelson & Sons Ltd 1989
Revised edition 1998

ISBN 0-17-411116-9
NPN 9 8 7 6 5 4 3 2 1
02 01 00 99 98

Designed and typeset by Ian Foulis & Associates
Printed in Croatia by Zrinski, Cakovec

Contents

1 Fill in the missing numbers.

Make each answer 20.

1. $\square \times 2 + 6$
2. $\square \div 3 + 13$
3. $\square \div 7 + 15$
4. $\square \times 5 - 5$
5. $\square \div 2 + 17$
6. $\square \times 6 - 16$
7. $3 \times 9 - \square$
8. $2 \times \square - 8$
9. $4 \times \square - 12$

2 Find the two numbers which have:

1. a total of 15 and a product of 56
2. a total of 13 and a product of 42
3. a total of 16 and a product of 63
4. a total of 18 and a product of 81
5. a total of 14 and a product of 45
6. a total of 14 and a product of 49
7. a total of 17 and a product of 72
8. a total of 16 and a product of 64

3 Put a number in each shape.

Shapes which are the same have the same number.

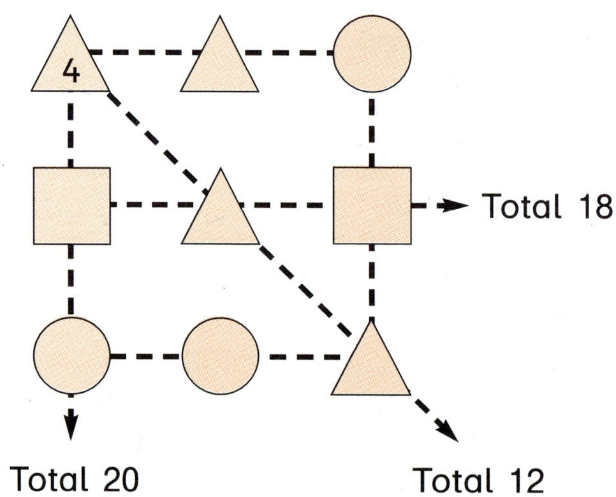

4 Work out each table fact.

Take the last letter of each answer, for example the 'y' of 'twenty'.

Write the word.						Clue
1.	4×2	9×9	$21 \div 3$	7×4		A camper uses one.
2.	$64 \div 8$	8×4	$70 \div 7$	10×3		A boy's name.
3.	10×10	9×8	7×6	6×4		It can be opened.
4.	$56 \div 8$	7×7	9×4	6×8		The one after.
5.	9×3	8×9	$80 \div 10$	9×7		A short letter.
6.	7×5	$49 \div 7$	$72 \div 9$	8×3	10×5	Way in.

5 Find the number.

1. It is an even number under 100.
   The digits total 5.
   It is a multiple of 7.

2. It is a square number.
   It is an odd number.
   The difference between its digits is 5.

3. It is an even number.
   It has twelve factors.
   It is a multiple of 8 and 9.
   It is under 100.

6 Use **odd** digits only.

Use +, −, × and ÷ as often as you wish.

Make these answers.

1. 15
2. 31
3. 40
4. 3
5. 33
6. 78
7. 36
8. 16
9. 26
10. 24

7 Find the missing number for each of these.

The **same number** is needed for **both boxes**.

1. 28 ÷ ☐ = ☐ r 3
2. 70 ÷ ☐ = ☐ r 6
3. 19 ÷ ☐ = ☐ r 3
4. 89 ÷ ☐ = ☐ r 8
5. 52 ÷ ☐ = ☐ r 3
6. 38 ÷ ☐ = ☐ r 2
7. 18 ÷ ☐ = ☐ r 2
8. 83 ÷ ☐ = ☐ r 2
9. 26 ÷ ☐ = ☐ r 1
10. 68 ÷ ☐ = ☐ r 4

8 Complete these.

1.

+		19	
	33	36	27
	30	33	24
	34	37	28

2.

−			11
	6	5	9
	2	1	5
	5	4	8

3.

×			
	14	8	12
	21	12	18
	35	20	30

9 Fit the digits 1, 2, 3 and 4 into the correct boxes.

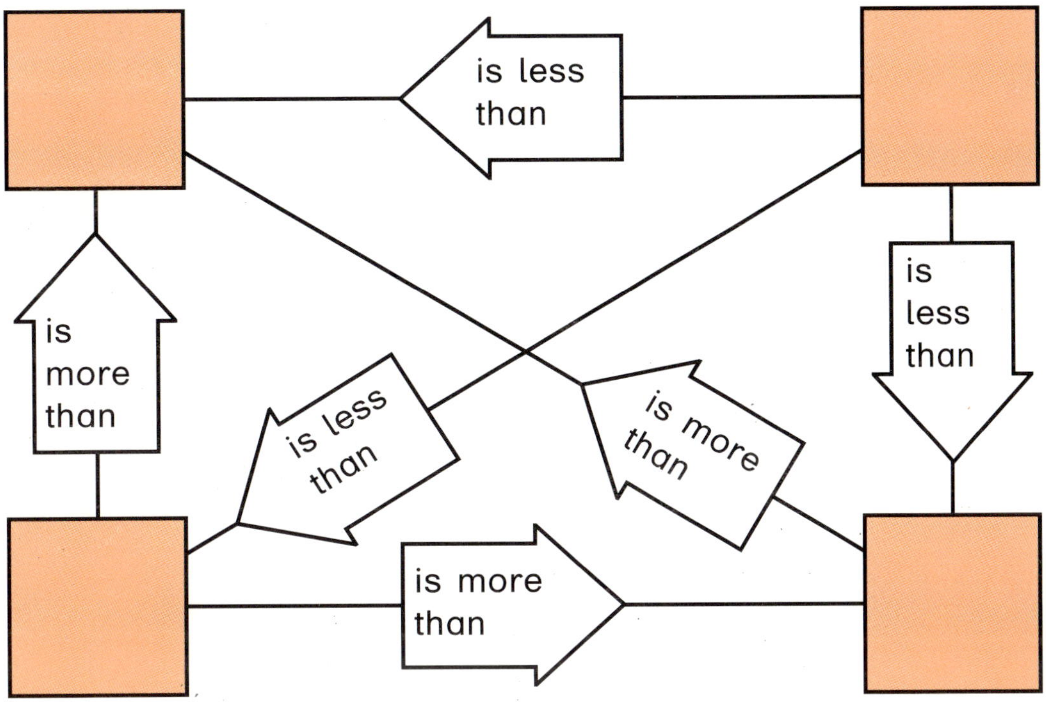

10

1.

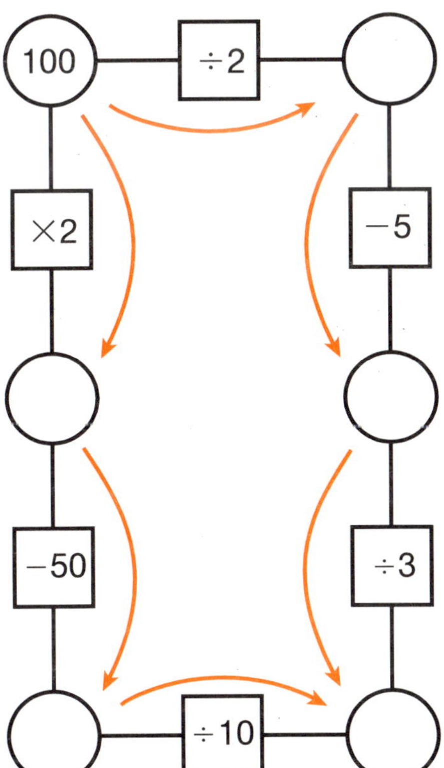

2.

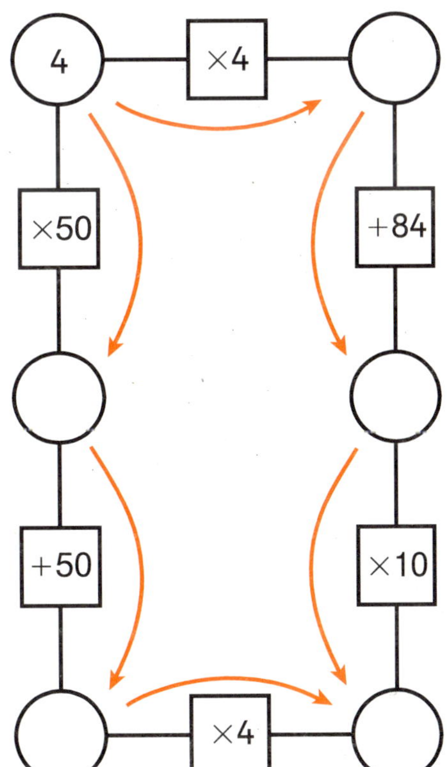

11 Do these as quickly as you can.

$5 \times \square = 20$	$\square \times 8 = 72$	$7 \times \square = 49$
$\square \times 9 = 54$	$6 \times \square = 24$	$3 \times \square = 15$
$7 \times 6 = \square$	$\square \times 4 = 28$	$6 \times 6 = \square$
$3 \times 9 = \square$	$7 \times 3 = \square$	$5 \times \square = 45$
$4 \times \square = 32$	$5 \times \square = 35$	$8 \times \square = 56$
$8 \times 5 = \square$	$6 \times \square = 42$	$\square \times 7 = 63$
$9 \times \square = 81$	$\square \times 8 = 48$	$8 \times \square = 64$

12

1. Take each of these from 100.

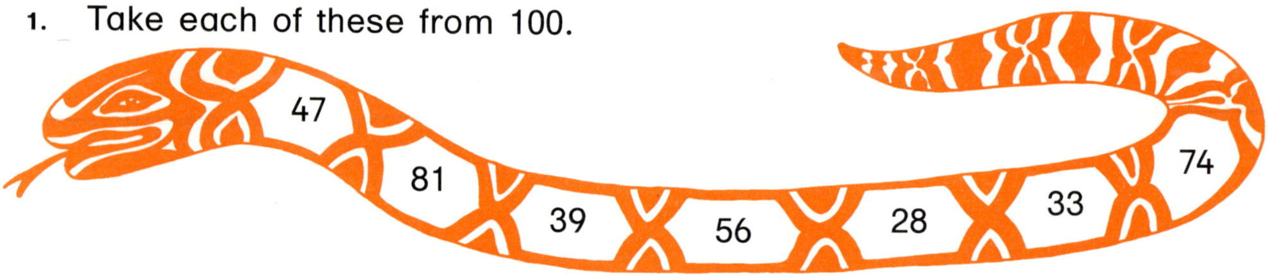

2. Take each of these from 1000.

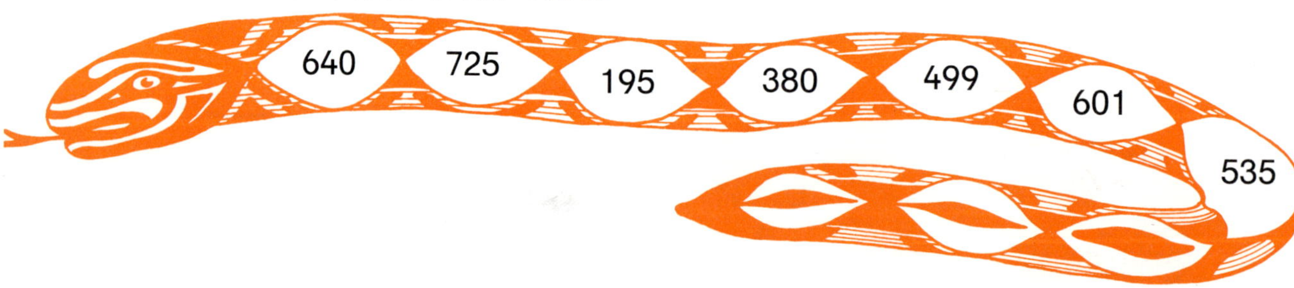

13 Try to do these in your head.

1. $12 + 32 + 18$
2. $55 + 45 + 70$
3. $199 + 199$
4. $8 \times 7 \times 10$
5. $99 + 99 + 99$
6. $158 + 72 - 157$
7. $999 + 137$
8. 24×20
9. $1001 - 99$
10. $750 + 299 + 250$
11. $286 + 199$
12. $260 - 61$

14

1. 26 × 10
   26 × 5
2. 48 × 10
   48 × 5
3. 18 × 10
   18 × 5
4. 52 × 10
   52 × 5
5. 62 × 10
   62 × 5
6. 76 × 10
   76 × 5
7. 34 × 10
   34 × 5
8. 88 × 10
   88 × 5
9. 74 × 10
   74 × 5

15 Find a half of:

1. 78
2. 246
3. 304
4. 170
5. £5
6. £4.50
7. £6.80
8. £3
9. 7 metres
10. 2·50 m
11. 4·20 m
12. 9 metres

16

1. Which pairs of numbers have a difference of 199?

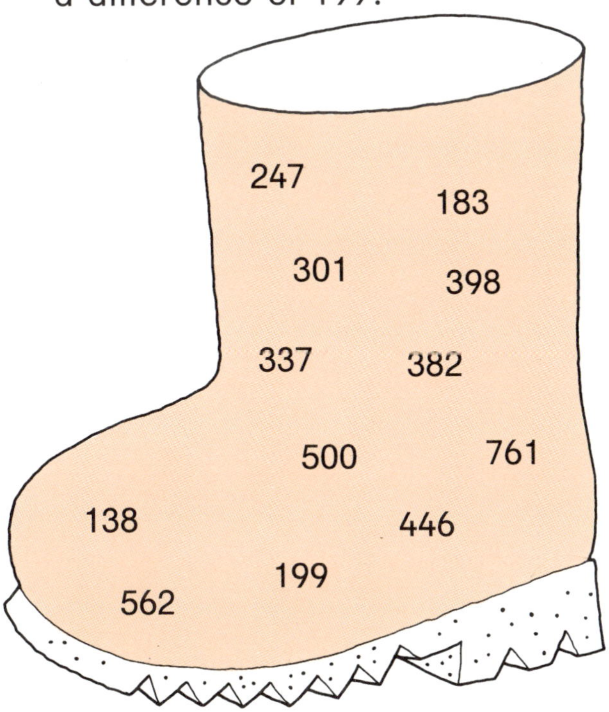

2. Find pairs of numbers where one is double the other.

17

1. 27 + 139

2. 416 + 298

3. 636 + 395

4. 409 + 729

5. 36 + 297 + 493

6. 504 + 79 + 379

7. 103 + 462 + 197

8. 694 + 386 + 96

9. 196 + 594

10. 628 + 278

11. 506 + 493 + 73

12. 446 + 293 + 108

18

1. Which of these add to give more than £10?

A £ 4.65 + 9.27

B £ 6.09 + 2.95

C £ 4.75 + 2.95

D £ 5.38 + 6.72

2. Which of these add to exactly 10 kg?

A kg 5·710 + 3·490

B kg 5·250 + 4·750

C kg 4·150 + 4·950

D kg 6·050 + 3·950

3. Which of these add to exactly 5 m?

A m 3·75 + 1·26

B m 2·68 + 2·32

C m 0·87 + 4·13

D m 1·59 + 3·51

19

1. 158
   −79

2. 270
   −148

3. 461
   −195

4. 307
   −188

5. 846
   −595

6. 600
   −58

7. 313
   −189

8. 508
   −379

9. 648 − 76

10. 813 − 496

11. Subtract 158 from 432.

12. Take 346 from 1702.

20 How much change from £10?

1. £6.45
2. £7.38
3. £0.54
4. £1.73
5. £5.05

Take each of these from 5 m.

6. 4·25 m
7. 135 cm
8. 4·75 m
9. 3·48 m
10. 205 cm

21 What must be added to make each of these into 3 kg?

1. 550 g
2. 1·240 kg
3. 1150 g
4. 2·775 kg
5. 1·995 kg

What must be added to make each of these into 5 l?

6. 1·600 l
7. 950 ml
8. 1·360 l
9. 1·180 l
10. 2·450 l

22

1. 16×4
2. 30×3
3. 16×8
4. 93×7
5. 117×5
6. 86×6
7. 408×2
8. 77×9
9. 178×10
10. 419×3
11. 297×5
12. 338×6
13. 478×7
14. 119×8
15. 161×9

23 Double each of these.

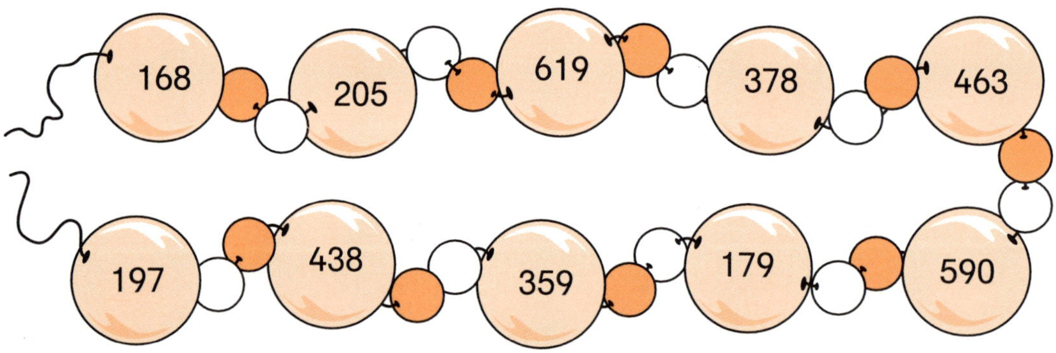

24 Multiply to find the answers.

1.
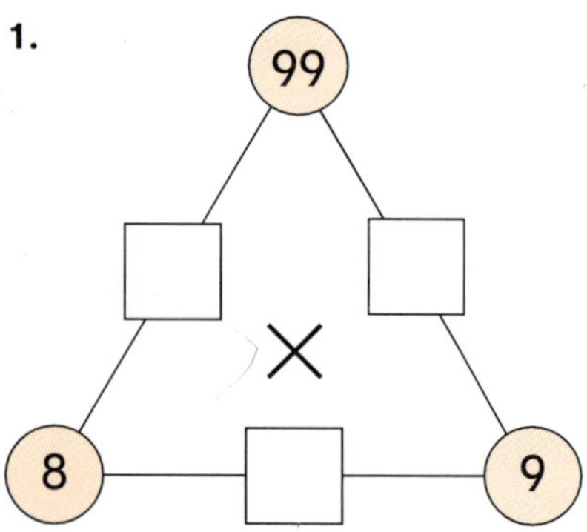

2.
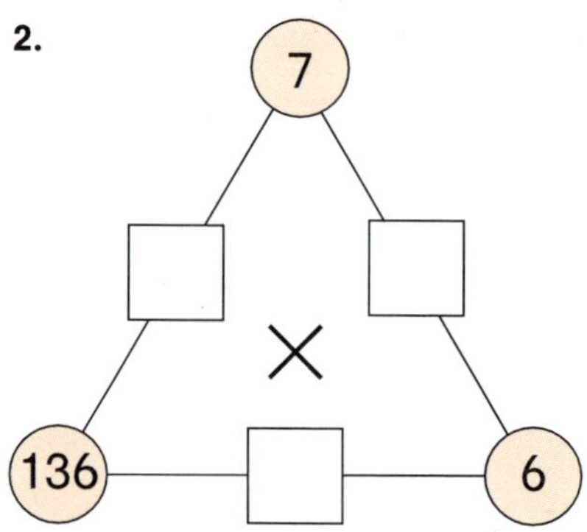

3.
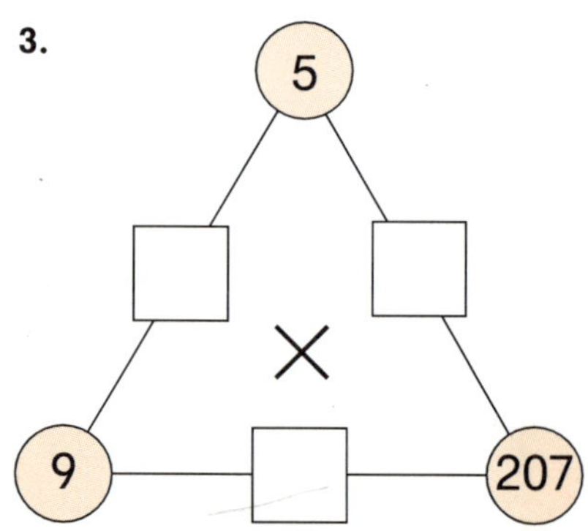

25

1. 5) 75
2. 6) 96
3. 7) 119
4. 8) 168
5. 4) 104
6. 9) 171
7. 6) 210
8. 8) 248
9. 2) 156
10. 5) 230
11. 3) 141
12. 7) 371

26 Find the average of each of these.

1. 260, 138, 73, 105
2. 36, 29, 111, 103, 71
3. 183, 201, 66, 102
4. 193, 215, 461, 38, 103
5. £1.45, £2.96, £2.01
6. £5.50, £3.68, £2.07, £3.39

27

Find $\frac{1}{3}$ of each of these.

1. 762
2. £1.41

Find $\frac{1}{4}$ of each of these.

5. 3·04 m
6. £5.76

Find $\frac{1}{2}$ of each of these.

3. 6512
4. £10.24

Find $\frac{1}{10}$ of each of these.

7. £8.60
8. 160 km

28 Which answers have a remainder that is an even number?

29 Five answers total 1000 when they are added together.

Which are they?

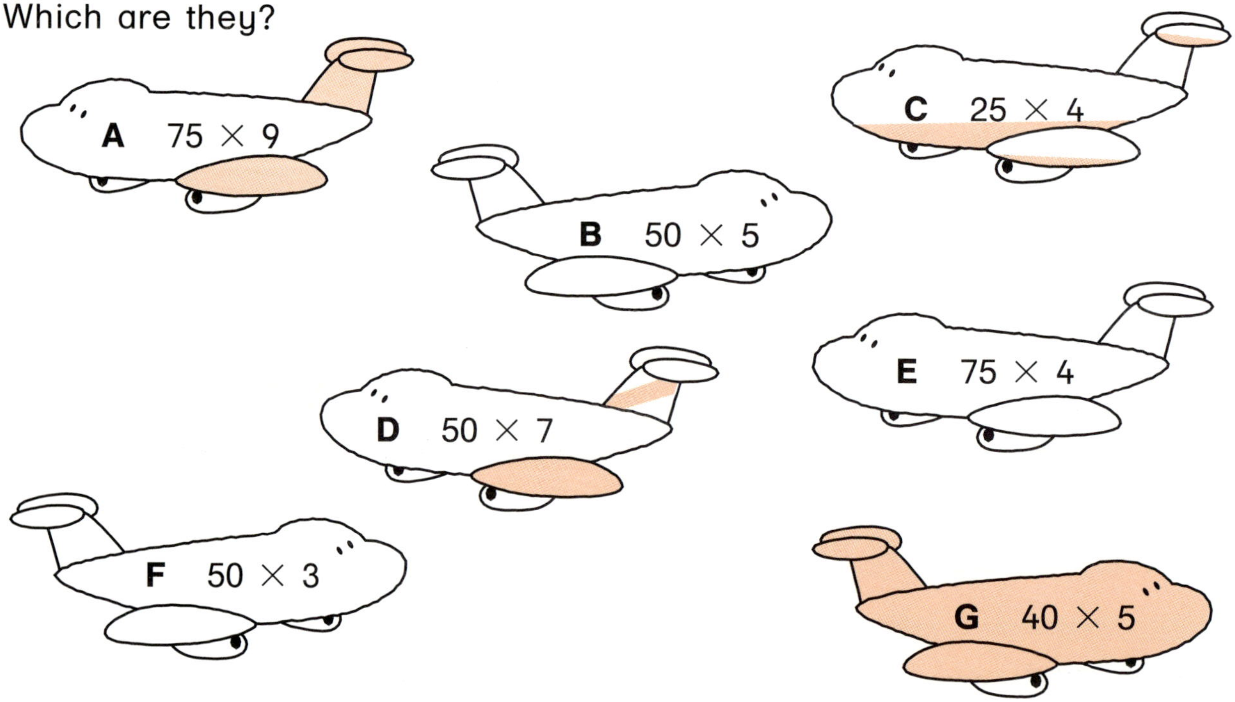

30 A car needs servicing after 10 000 miles.

How many more miles before the next service?

1. 0 4 3 2 5
2. 0 1 3 4 1
3. 0 7 9 0 3
4. 0 4 3 7 5
5. 0 9 3 8 8
6. 0 2 4 6 5

31 Find the next three missing numbers.

1.	156	196	236	276			
2.	863	793	723	653			
3.	241	220	199	178			
4.	278	304	330	356			

32 Which do you think gives the smallest answer in each group?

Check whether you were right.

33 Match each statement with its answer.

1. $4 \times (7 - 2)$
2. $(13 \times 3) - 5$
3. $36 - (18 - 6)$
4. $(50 \div 10) + 6$
5. $13 \times (9 - 5)$
6. $26 \div (17 - 15)$
7. $(6 \times 4) + (3 \times 9)$
8. $(28 \div 4) - (15 - 9)$
9. $(7 \times 5) - (15 - 9)$
10. $8 \times (6 + 3) \div 9$

34 51 52 8 20 29 1 11 13 24

34 Which gives the answer nearest to 100?

A $(17 \times 4) + 25$

B $15 \times (4 + 3)$

C $(18 - 9) \times 10$

D $125 - (17 + 6)$

E $(26 + 24) + (100 - 44)$

F $(92 + 102) \div (6 \div 3)$

G $115 - (35 - 26)$

H $(7 \times 7) + (12 \times 4)$

I $26 \times (27 - 23)$

35 Use brackets to make each answer zero.

1. $27 - 9 \times 3$
2. $100 - 50 + 50$
3. $32 \div 8 - 4$
4. $6 \times 4 \times 7 - 7$
5. $16 + 4 - 2 \times 10$
6. $25 \div 5 - 6 - 1$
7. $16 + 3 - 24 - 5$
8. $14 \times 3 - 2 - 14$
9. $4 \times 2 + 3 - 20$

36 Use brackets to make each answer a multiple of 10.

1. $8 + 3 \times 4$
2. $7 \times 12 + 8$
3. $74 - 16 + 28$
4. $47 - 28 - 11$
5. $14 \times 6 + 26$
6. $7 \times 3 + 7$
7. $28 - 7 + 1$
8. $6 \times 4 + 3 \times 2$
9. $18 - 7 \times 2 + 26$

37 Fill in the missing numbers.

They are all multiples of 4.

1. $(16 + 8) \times \square = 192$
2. $21 - (34 - \square) = 19$
3. $(7 \times \square) - 6 = 50$
4. $\square - (16 - 9) = 41$
5. $(100 - \square) \times 2 = 72$
6. $(\square + 16) - 28 = 12$
7. $8 \times (\square - 3) = 72$
8. $74 - (\square + 5) = 21$
9. $25 - (\square \div 4) = 21$
10. $(3 + \square) - 10 = 21$

38 Use brackets to make each answer as small as possible.

1. $4 \times 6 - 3$
2. $17 - 12 + 4$
3. $9 \times 9 - 4$
4. $28 - 16 - 4$
5. $13 + 17 \times 2$
6. $17 - 3 \times 4$
7. $4 \times 6 - 3 + 2$
8. $22 - 7 - 5 + 3$
9. $7 \times 8 - 4 + 3$

39

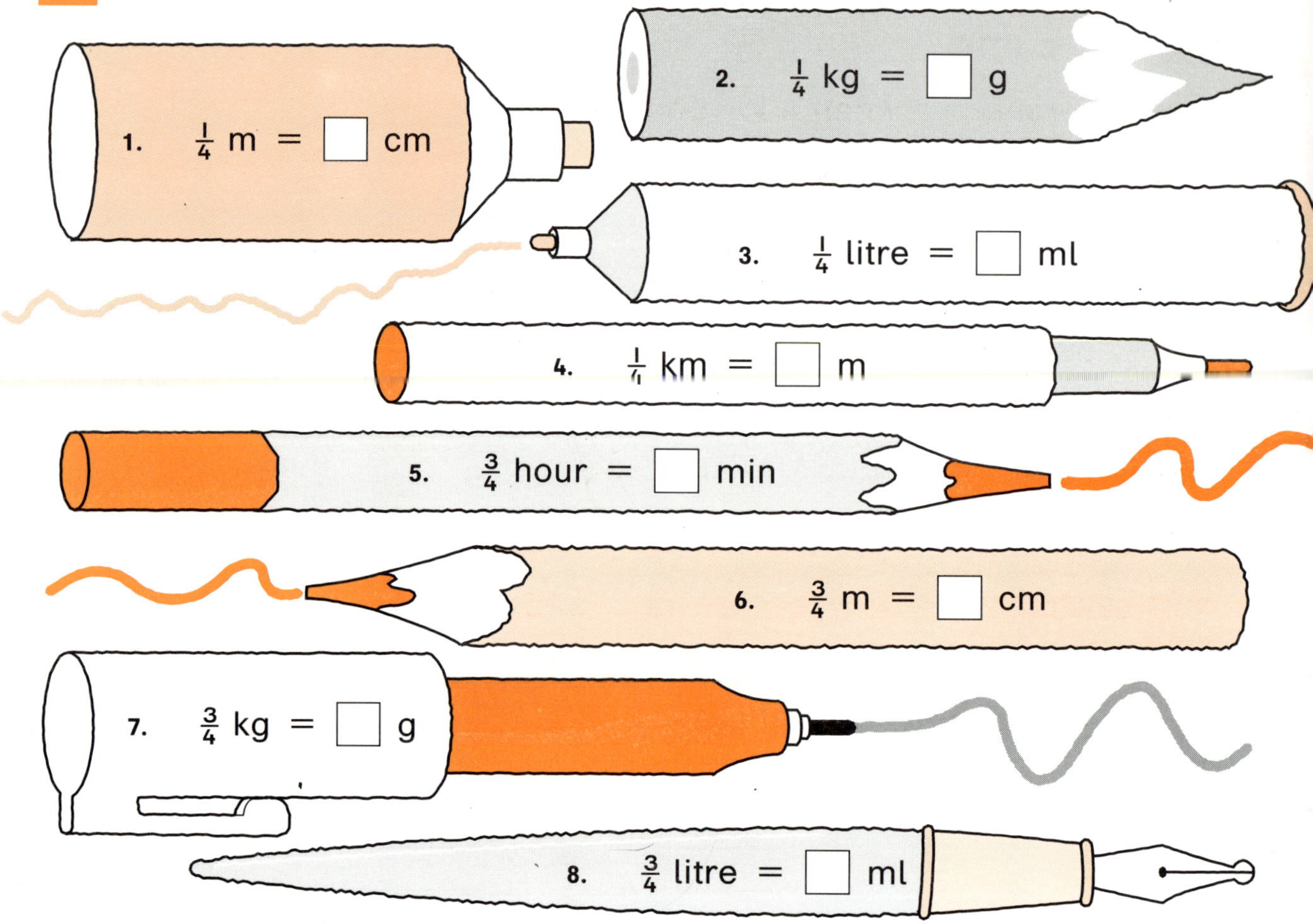

1. $\frac{1}{4}$ m = ☐ cm
2. $\frac{1}{4}$ kg = ☐ g
3. $\frac{1}{4}$ litre = ☐ ml
4. $\frac{1}{4}$ km = ☐ m
5. $\frac{3}{4}$ hour = ☐ min
6. $\frac{3}{4}$ m = ☐ cm
7. $\frac{3}{4}$ kg = ☐ g
8. $\frac{3}{4}$ litre = ☐ ml

40 Which gives the greatest answer?

A $\frac{1}{3}$ of 69

B $\frac{1}{4}$ of 56

C $\frac{3}{4}$ of 32

D $\frac{1}{2}$ of 38

E $\frac{3}{5}$ of 35

F $\frac{7}{10}$ of 30

41 Put in the sign >, < or =.

1. $\frac{1}{2}$ ☐ $\frac{4}{8}$
2. $\frac{1}{2}$ ☐ $\frac{2}{3}$
3. $\frac{2}{5}$ ☐ $\frac{1}{2}$
4. $\frac{2}{3}$ ☐ $\frac{3}{4}$
5. $\frac{2}{10}$ ☐ $\frac{3}{5}$
6. $\frac{2}{3}$ ☐ $\frac{9}{10}$
7. $\frac{5}{8}$ ☐ $\frac{1}{2}$
8. $\frac{1}{8}$ ☐ $\frac{1}{4}$

42 Double each of these.

1. $\frac{3}{4}$ 2. $1\frac{1}{2}$ 3. $1\frac{1}{5}$ 4. $2\frac{1}{4}$ 5. $\frac{7}{10}$

Find the difference between each pair of fractions.

6. $(\frac{3}{4}, \frac{1}{2})$ 7. $(1\frac{1}{2}, \frac{3}{4})$ 8. $(\frac{3}{8}, \frac{1}{4})$ 9. $(\frac{4}{5}, \frac{1}{5})$ 10. $(\frac{1}{2}, \frac{3}{10})$

43 What is the value of:

1. $\frac{1}{4}$ of £2.60
2. $\frac{1}{3}$ of £3.90
3. $\frac{1}{3}$ of £1.80
4. $\frac{3}{4}$ of £3.80
5. $\frac{1}{5}$ of £7
6. $\frac{1}{5}$ of £6.40
7. $\frac{1}{2}$ of £4.70
8. $\frac{2}{3}$ of £7.50
9. $\frac{1}{10}$ of £6.40
10. $\frac{3}{4}$ of £1.20

44 How many ml in each?

1.

2.

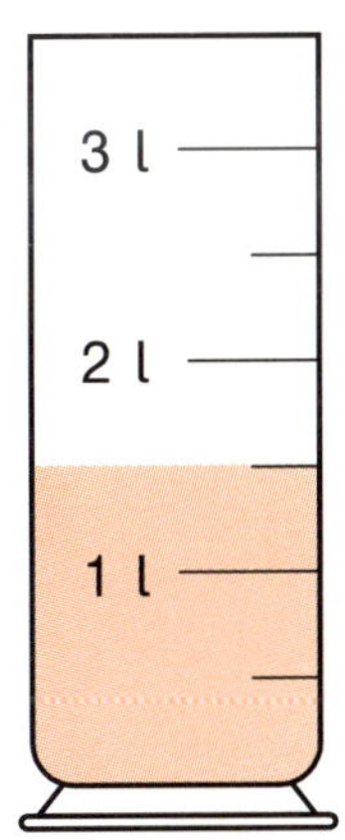

3.

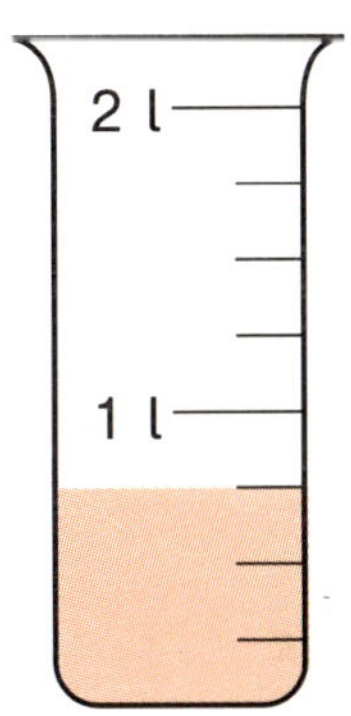

4.

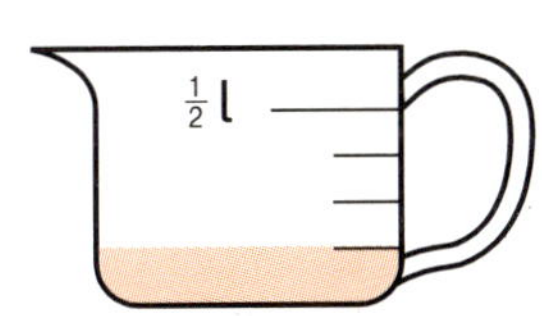

45 Write the pairs of fractions which total 1.

$\frac{1}{2}, \frac{3}{4}$ $\frac{3}{4}, \frac{1}{4}$ $\frac{1}{2}, \frac{1}{2}$ $\frac{1}{5}, \frac{7}{10}$

$\frac{1}{3}, \frac{4}{6}$ $\frac{1}{3}, \frac{1}{2}$ $\frac{1}{2}, \frac{5}{10}$

$\frac{9}{10}, \frac{1}{5}$ $\frac{4}{10}, \frac{3}{5}$

46 Write each line of fractions in order of size.

Start with the smallest.

1. $\frac{1}{8}$ $\frac{3}{4}$ $\frac{5}{8}$ $\frac{1}{4}$
2. $\frac{2}{5}$ $\frac{7}{10}$ $\frac{4}{5}$ $\frac{3}{10}$
3. $\frac{1}{2}$ $\frac{1}{3}$ $\frac{1}{4}$ $\frac{2}{3}$
4. $\frac{3}{5}$ $\frac{1}{2}$ $\frac{9}{10}$ $\frac{1}{5}$
5. $\frac{1}{4}$ $\frac{1}{2}$ $\frac{1}{8}$ $\frac{1}{3}$
6. $\frac{1}{4}$ $\frac{1}{10}$ $\frac{1}{2}$ $\frac{9}{10}$

47 Which fraction is under each blot?

1. ▬ of 24 is 12
2. ▬ of 28 is 7
3. ▬ of 100 is 10
4. ▬ of 32 is 4
5. ▬ of 12 is 9
6. ▬ of 30 is 10
7. ▬ of 15 is 10
8. ▬ of 18 is 3
9. ▬ of 20 is 4
10. ▬ of 50 is 20

48 Rearrange these to make decimal numbers less than 1.

1. · 6 4 0
2. 7 0 · 3
3. 2 0 ·
4. 5 0 · 3
5. 0 8 2 ·
6. · 4 4 0

49 Rearrange these to make decimal numbers between 1 and 5.

1. 8 · 4
2. 7 4 ·
3. · 4 9
4. 3 5 · 9
5. 6 7 · 2
6. 5 1 · 0

50 Rearrange these to make numbers between $\frac{1}{2}$ and $1\frac{1}{2}$.

1. 6 3 1 ·
2. · 0 1 4
3. · 7 0 7
4. 4 · 0 9
5. 6 · 1 4
6. 7 · 0 9

51 Rearrange these to make the number nearest to 5.

1. 3 7 .
2. 6 3 .
3. . 7 2
4. 1 8 .
5. 6 . 9
6. . 4 6

52 Rearrange these to make the number nearest to 7.

1. 8 . 5
2. 4 . 9
3. . 4 7
4. 2 . 1
5. 6 . 1 4
6. 1 3 1 .

53 Rearrange these to make the number nearest to 10.

1. . 7 9 1
2. 2 1 8 .
3. 1 . 1 9
4. . 3 2 1
5. . 6 3 1
6. 9 7 . 8

54 Put each set of decimal numbers in order of size.
Start with the smallest each time.

1. 1·3, 1·25, 1·7, 1·9, 0·9, 1·34
2. 2·6, 3·1, 1·99, 2·75, 3·08, 2·1
3. 0·75, 1·06, 0·9, 1·1, 0·82, 0·81
4. 4·06, 2·9, 5·1, 3·61, 3·8, 4·05
5. 7·96, 10·1, 8·07, 8·92, 8·1

55 Add the smallest number possible to make each of these a whole number.

1.	6·4	2.	12·7	3.	1·38	4.	24·81
5.	14·8	6.	12·09	7.	17·3	8.	9·05
9.	13·65	10.	18·6	11.	15·69	12.	19·99

56 Write the missing numbers halfway along the number line.

1. 1 □ 2
2. 7 □ 10
3. 5·5 □ 6·5
4. 2·4 □ 2·6
5. 1·5 □ 1·6
6. 0·1 □ 0·5
7. 3 □ 12
8. 3·4 □ 3·8
9. 4·6 □ 4·7
10. 2·5 □ 3

57

1. $\begin{array}{r} 5{\cdot}83 \\ +2{\cdot}07 \\ \hline \\ \hline \end{array}$

2. $\begin{array}{r} 3{\cdot}8 \\ +4{\cdot}79 \\ \hline \\ \hline \end{array}$

3. $\begin{array}{r} 5{\cdot}83 \\ +7{\cdot}96 \\ \hline \\ \hline \end{array}$

4. $\begin{array}{r} 3{\cdot}49 \\ +1{\cdot}97 \\ \hline \\ \hline \end{array}$

5. $\begin{array}{r} 3{\cdot}4 \\ 0{\cdot}78 \\ +2{\cdot}45 \\ \hline \\ \hline \end{array}$

6. $\begin{array}{r} 1{\cdot}78 \\ 0{\cdot}84 \\ +6{\cdot}9 \\ \hline \\ \hline \end{array}$

7. $\begin{array}{r} 5{\cdot}78 \\ 3{\cdot}6 \\ +7{\cdot}1 \\ \hline \\ \hline \end{array}$

8. $\begin{array}{r} 0{\cdot}07 \\ 0{\cdot}8 \\ +\ 0{\cdot}45 \\ \hline \\ \hline \end{array}$

9. 1·62 + 2·9 + 3·48

10. 3·6 + 1·95 + 2·88

58 Put these in order of size, beginning with the largest.

1. 3·2 3·17 3·199 3·204
2. 2·042 2·1 2·202 2·194
3. 7·59 7·6 7·599 7·09
4. 4·1 3·9 3·899 3·09
5. 1·05 0·95 1·005 1·1
6. 7·095 6·91 6·905 7·13

59

1. $\begin{array}{r} 3{\cdot}24 \\ -1{\cdot}98 \\ \hline \\ \hline \end{array}$

2. $\begin{array}{r} 7{\cdot}09 \\ -4{\cdot}68 \\ \hline \\ \hline \end{array}$

3. $\begin{array}{r} 1{\cdot}09 \\ -0{\cdot}92 \\ \hline \\ \hline \end{array}$

4. $\begin{array}{r} 3{\cdot}45 \\ -0{\cdot}76 \\ \hline \\ \hline \end{array}$

5. $\begin{array}{r} 8{\cdot}7 \\ -4{\cdot}98 \\ \hline \\ \hline \end{array}$

6. $\begin{array}{r} 2{\cdot}72 \\ -0{\cdot}9 \\ \hline \\ \hline \end{array}$

7. $\begin{array}{r} 4{\cdot}03 \\ -1{\cdot}77 \\ \hline \\ \hline \end{array}$

8. $\begin{array}{r} 8{\cdot}2 \\ -1{\cdot}74 \\ \hline \\ \hline \end{array}$

9. 6·4 − 3·67

10. 1·5 − 0·73

60 Put the numbers in the correct boxes.

1. ☐ > ☐ > ☐ 0·75 3·075 0·025

2. ☐ < ☐ < ☐ 2·35 2·079 2·111

3. ☐ < ☐ < ☐ 4 0·999 3·7

4. ☐ > ☐ > ☐ 6·01 6·001 6·1

5. ☐ > ☐ > ☐ 17·42 7·999 17·1

6. ☐ < ☐ < ☐ 0·06 0·049 0·072

61

1. Find pairs of decimal numbers where one is half the other.

1·9 5·2 3·8 4·6 3·3 2·6 2·3 1·65

2. Find pairs of numbers where one is four times the other.

1·3 5·2 1·5 10·4 7·6 1·25 5 6 2·6 1·9

62 Find the missing decimal points.

1. 46 + 37 = 8·3
2. 46 + 37 = 49·7
3. 46 + 37 = 4·16
4. 46 + 37 = 41·6
5. 46 + 37 = 4·97
6. 46 − 37 = 0·9
7. 46 − 37 = 42·3
8. 46 − 37 = 4·23
9. 46 − 37 = 45·63
10. 46 − 37 = 0·09

63 Which decimal numbers do the arrows point to?

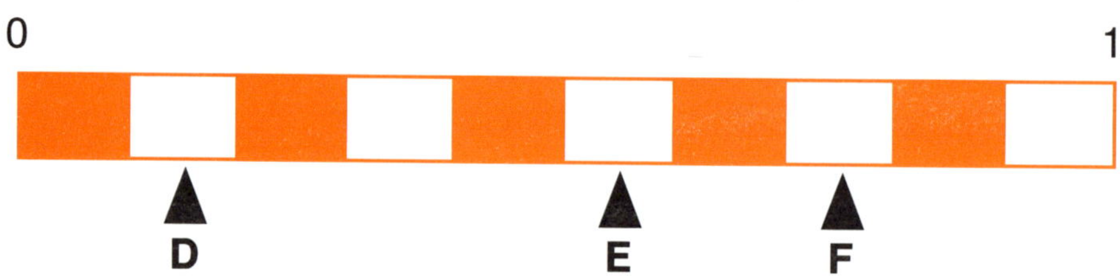

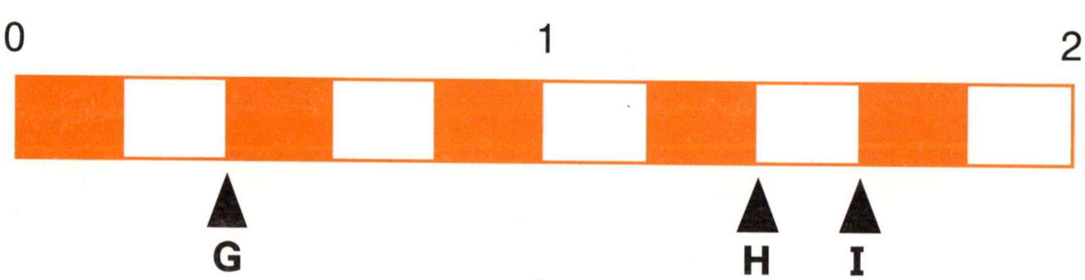

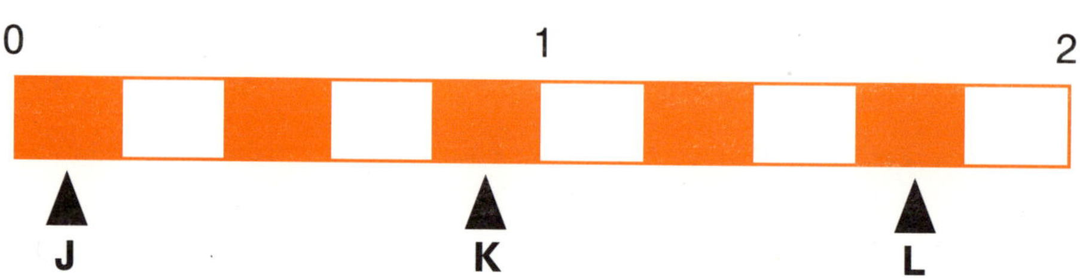

64 What has each been multiplied or divided by?

1. 2·4 ——→ 0·24
2. 0·5 ——→ 50
3. 1·7 ←—— 170
4. 3·8 ←—— 38
5. 0·74 ——→ 74
6. 0·42 ——→ 4·2
7. 1·74 ——→ 174
8. 130 ——→ 1·3

65

Divide each of these by 10.

1. 4·5
2. 174
3. 0·9
4. 1·6
5 13·4

Divide each of these by 100.

6. 180
7. 17
8. 910
9. 472
10. 1200

66

1.

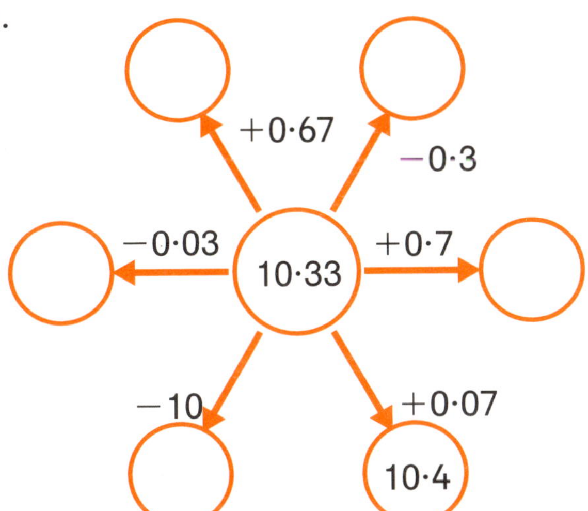

2.

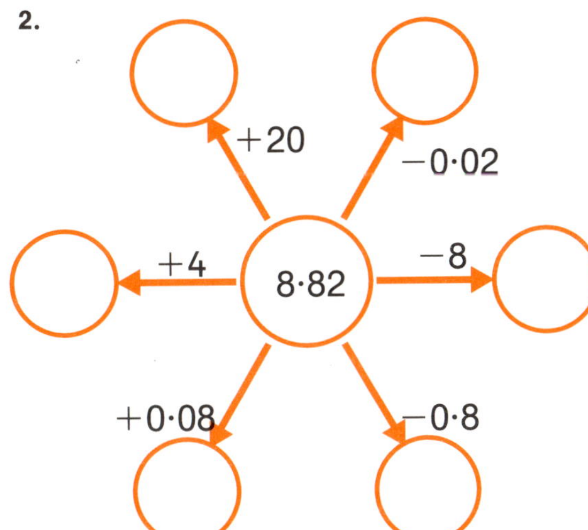

67 Which is the best buy?

1.

2.

3.

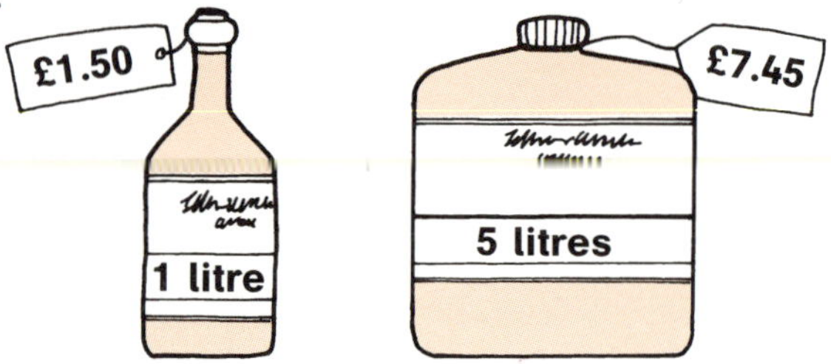

4.

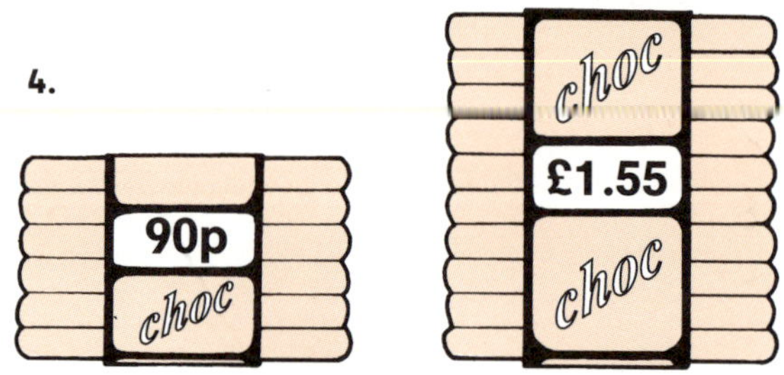

5.

6.

68 This area has to be tiled.

1. Which of these tiles will fit without being cut?

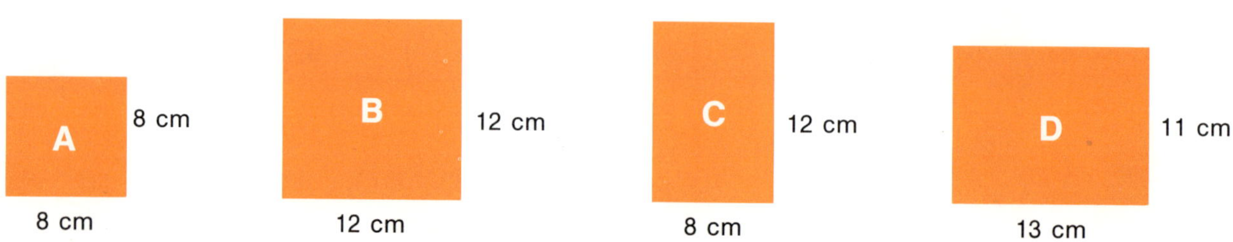

2. How many of each would be needed?

69 The centre total is 100.

Can you see how it was found?
Pairs in the outer ring were multiplied.
Numbers in the inner ring were added.

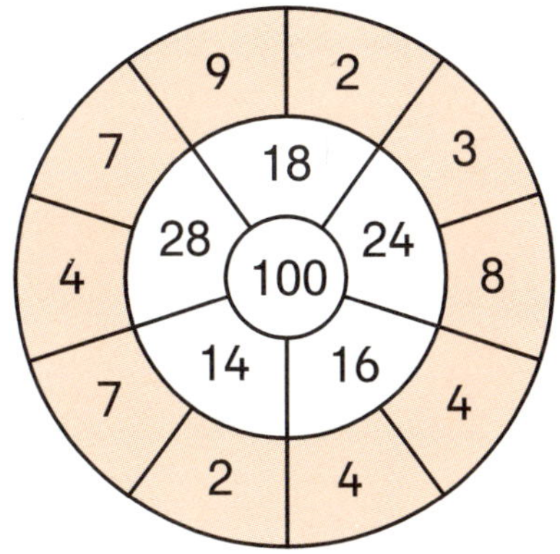

Find the centre total for these.

1.

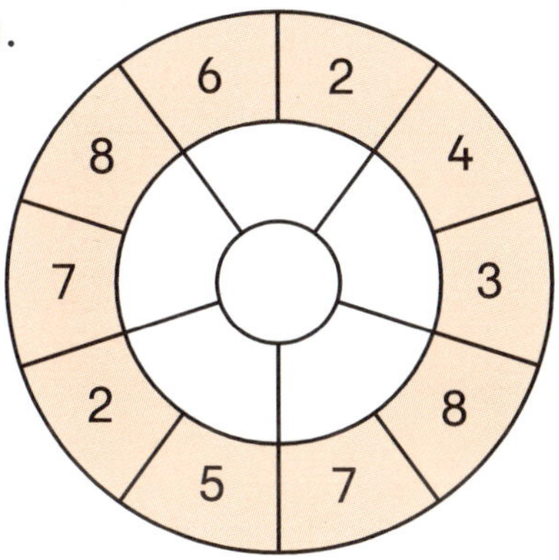

2.

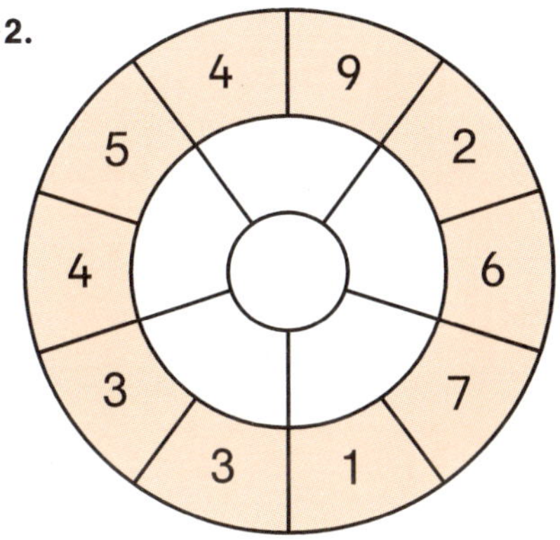

3.

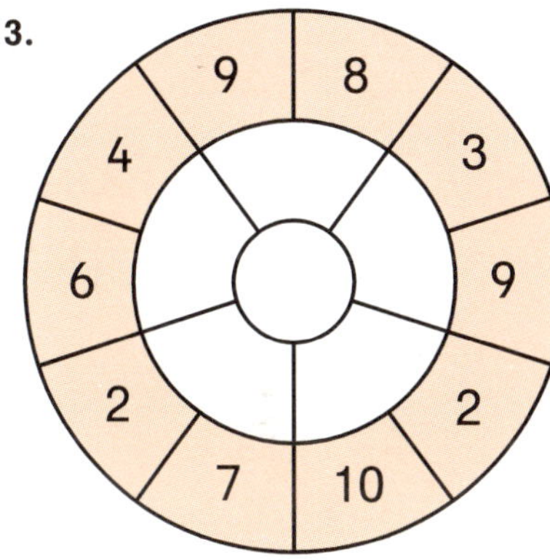

4.

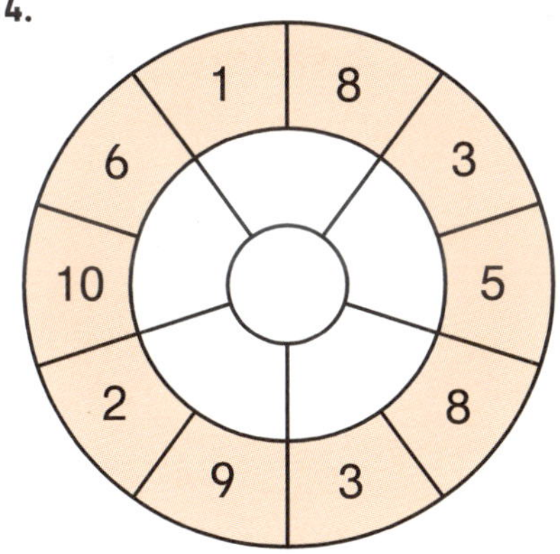

5.

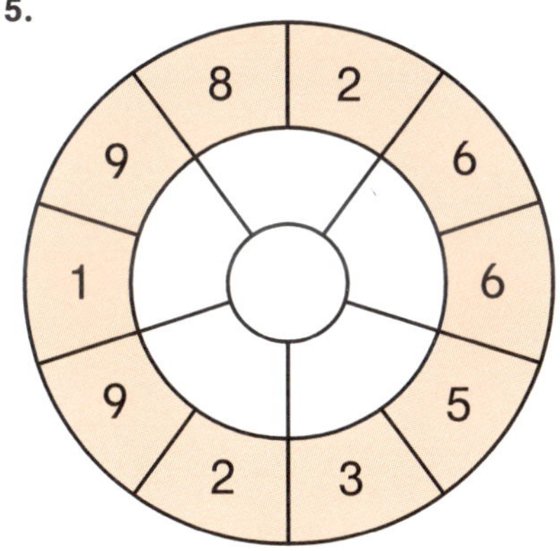

6.

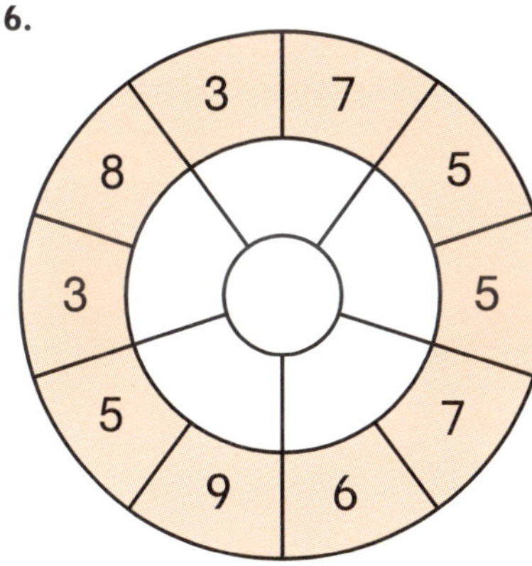

70 Find all the multiples of 8 among these numbers.

Total them.

64	79	114	128	192	32
36	24	150	144	160	98
48	136	56	102	138	16

71 In one week 3948 people visited the Railway Museum.

1876 of these visited it on a weekday.

1. How many visited it at the weekend?
2. The cost of entrance was 50p per person.
   How much money was collected that week?

72 Electricity used is measured in units.

The number of units is shown on a dial.

The dial in August showed

The dial in November showed

1. How many units were used between August and November?
2. Each unit costs 10p.
   What is the cost of the electricity used?

73 How much is saved on each car?

74 This table shows the times of some trains from Crewe to London.

Crewe dep.	0709	0753	1110	1312	1513	1804	1910
Rugby	0809	↓	1211	1408	1609	↓	2006
London arr.	0915	0946	1326	1521	1715	2013	2115

1. Which trains do not stop at Rugby?
2. Which is the first train to reach London in the afternoon?
3. Which train does the journey in the shortest time?
4. Which train takes longest for the journey?
5. Which two trains take the same time for the journey?
6. What is the latest train you could catch at Rugby to reach London by 4 pm?

75 Start at 6. How many routes can you find that give you totals over 100?

You can only move one square up or one square to the right each time.

9	8	17	7
13	15	22	11
19	14	12	16
6	11	28	5

76

1. $\square \xrightarrow{\times 8} 96$
2. $\square \xrightarrow{\div 7} 11$
3. $\square \xrightarrow{+36} 85$
4. $\square \xrightarrow{-29} 63$
5. $\square \xrightarrow{\times 5} 75$
6. $\square \xrightarrow{\div 9} 12$
7. $\square \xrightarrow{+25} 59$
8. $\square \xrightarrow{-54} 99$
9. $\square \xrightarrow{\times 6} 84$
10. $\square \xrightarrow{\div 8} 17$
11. $\square \xrightarrow{+64} 129$
12. $\square \xrightarrow{-48} 29$

77 The digits 0 to 9 are missing from these problems.

Each digit can only be used once.

Can you find where they go?

$4 + \square = 7$ $\quad \square - \square = 9$ $\quad 5 + \square = \square$

$\square - \square = \square$ $\quad 4 + \square = \square$

78

1. $23 \xrightarrow{\times 4} \square$
2. $54 \xrightarrow{+ \square} 87$
3. $\square \xrightarrow{\div 5} 17$
4. $144 \xrightarrow{\div 8} \square$
5. $86 \xrightarrow{- \square} 19$
6. $\square \xrightarrow{\times 4} 60$
7. $97 \xrightarrow{+26} \square$
8. $25 \xrightarrow{\times \square} 125$
9. $\square \xrightarrow{+35} 100$
10. $203 \xrightarrow{-46} \square$
11. $81 \xrightarrow{\div \square} 9$
12. $\square \xrightarrow{-42} 68$

79 Which numbers will come out of the Function Machines?

1.

2.

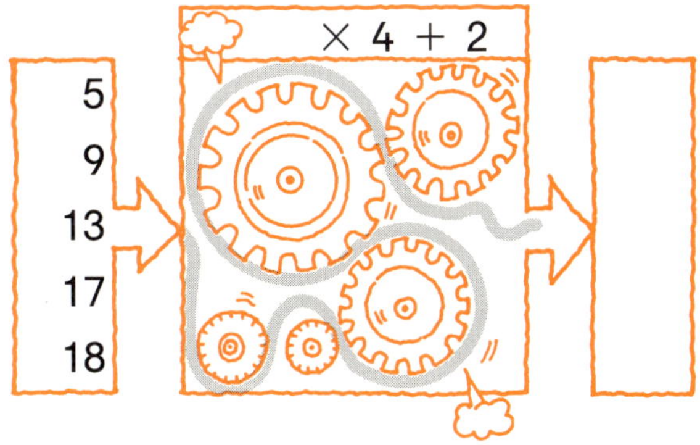

3.

4.

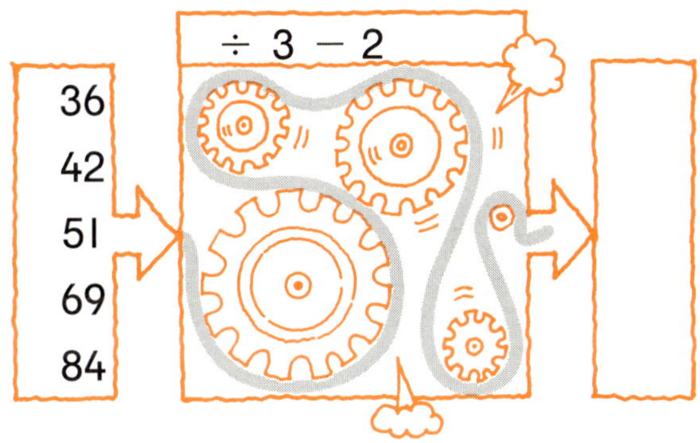

80 Which numbers were fed into the Function Machines?

1.

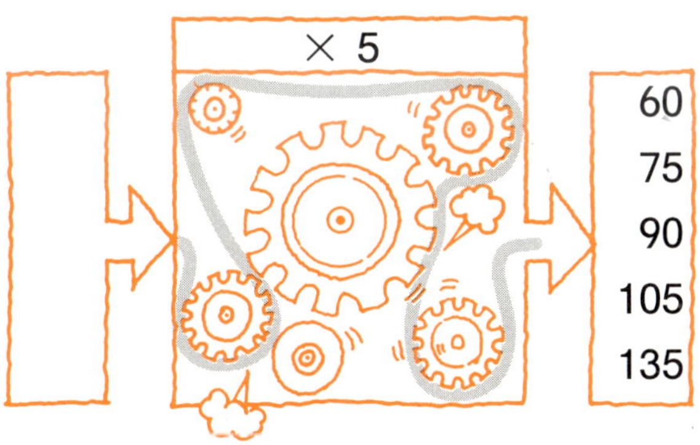

2.

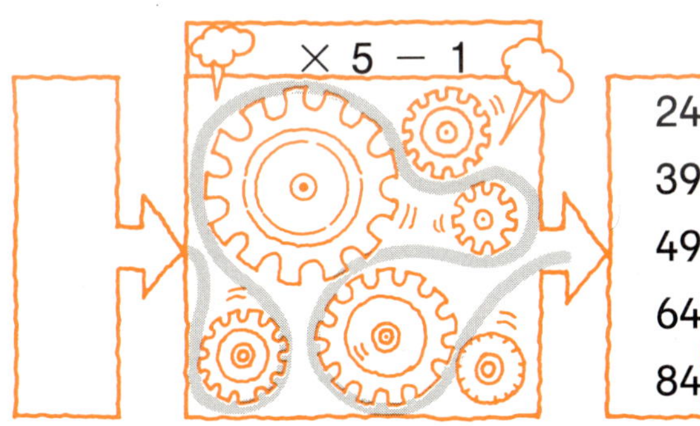

3.

4.

81

1. $8 \xrightarrow{\times \square} 136$
2. $27 \xrightarrow{+ \square} 95$
3. $87 \xrightarrow{- \square} 38$
4. $128 \xrightarrow{\div \square} 8$
5. $12 \xrightarrow{\times \square} 108$
6. $87 \xrightarrow{+ \square} 123$
7. $99 \xrightarrow{- \square} 46$
8. $72 \xrightarrow{\div \square} 9$
9. $11 \xrightarrow{\times \square} 99$
10. $54 \xrightarrow{+ \square} 123$
11. $126 \xrightarrow{- \square} 37$
12. $121 \xrightarrow{\div \square} 11$

82 Find the numbers.

1. The product of two numbers is 60.
Their difference is 7.
What are the numbers?
2. The total of two numbers is 24.
One number is twice as big as the other.
What are the numbers?
3. Two numbers have a product of 72.
One number is half the other.
What are the numbers?
4. A number is halved and then halved again.
The answer is 8.
What is the number?
5. The total of three numbers is 21.
The first number is twice as big as the second.
The second number is twice as big as the third.
What are the numbers?

83

1. $\begin{array}{r} 4{*}7 \\ +235 \\ \hline 72{*} \\ \hline \end{array}$

2. $\begin{array}{r} {*}35 \\ 24{*} \\ +155 \\ \hline 7{*}6 \\ \hline \end{array}$

3. $\begin{array}{r} 436 \\ {*}{*}4 \\ +\ 4{*} \\ \hline 875 \\ \hline \end{array}$

4. $\begin{array}{r} {*}3{*} \\ 504 \\ +1{*}6 \\ \hline 890 \\ \hline \end{array}$

5. $\begin{array}{r} 235 \\ {*}1{*} \\ +2{*}7 \\ \hline 896 \\ \hline \end{array}$

6. $\begin{array}{r} 4{*}3 \\ -14{*} \\ \hline 335 \\ \hline \end{array}$

7. $\begin{array}{r} {*}42 \\ -1{*}{*} \\ \hline 375 \\ \hline \end{array}$

8. $\begin{array}{r} 3{*}{*} \\ -142 \\ \hline {*}58 \\ \hline \end{array}$

9. $\begin{array}{r} 5{*}8 \\ -{*}4{*} \\ \hline 260 \\ \hline \end{array}$

10. $\begin{array}{r} 4{*}{*} \\ -{*}47 \\ \hline 177 \\ \hline \end{array}$

84 Fill in the missing numbers.

1. $\frac{1}{2}$ of $\square$ is 24.
2. $\frac{1}{3}$ of $\square$ is 8.
3. $\frac{3}{4}$ of $\square$ is 12.
4. $\frac{1}{6}$ of $\square$ is 10.
5. Double $\square$ is 122.
6. Double $\square$ is 3.
7. $(7 \times \square) + 13 = 27$
8. $(6 + 4) + (2 \times \square) = 30$
9. $\square$ less than 80 is 55.
10. $\square$ more than 38 is 57.
11. A quarter of $\square$ is 35.
12. Three-quarters of $\square$ is 18.

85

1. $7 \times 9 = 50 + \square$
2. $\square - 36 = 5 \times 6$
3. $48 \div \square = 54 - 48$
4. $18 + \square = 66 - 26$
5. $25 \times \square = 256 - 156$
6. $102 - 95 = 84 \div \square$
7. $70 - 14 = 7 \times \square$
8. $9 \times 8 = \square + 56$
9. $4 \times 9 = 17 + \square$
10. $\square + 49 = 7 \times 9$
11. $47 - 38 = \square \div 6$
12. $36 \div \square = 72 \div 8$

86 Use brackets to make each answer a **prime number**.

1. $12 - 2 + 5$
2. $6 \times 3 + 1$
3. $30 - 14 - 1$
4. $7 + 4 + 9 \times 2$
5. $4 + 5 \times 2 + 5$
6. $6 \times 5 - 1 \times 7$
7. $2 \times 12 - 7 + 3$
8. $7 + 15 - 6 + 5$
9. $2 \times 8 + 7$

87 What must be added to each of these to make the next **square number**?

1. 17
2. 29
3. 38
4. 11
5. 55
6. 65
7. 92
8. 5
9. 79

88 Use the digits 1, 3, 4, 6, 7 and 8.

The total of each side is a **triangular number**.

Find a home for each digit.

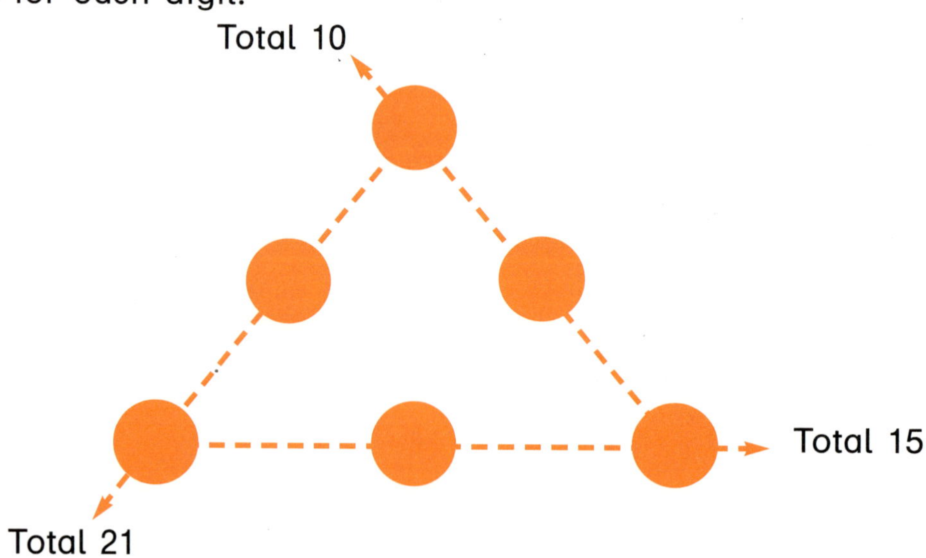

89 Add three **consecutive numbers** to give an answer:

1. between 80 and 90
2. nearest to 100
3. which has only the digit 1 in it.

90 1. Divide each of these numbers by 7.

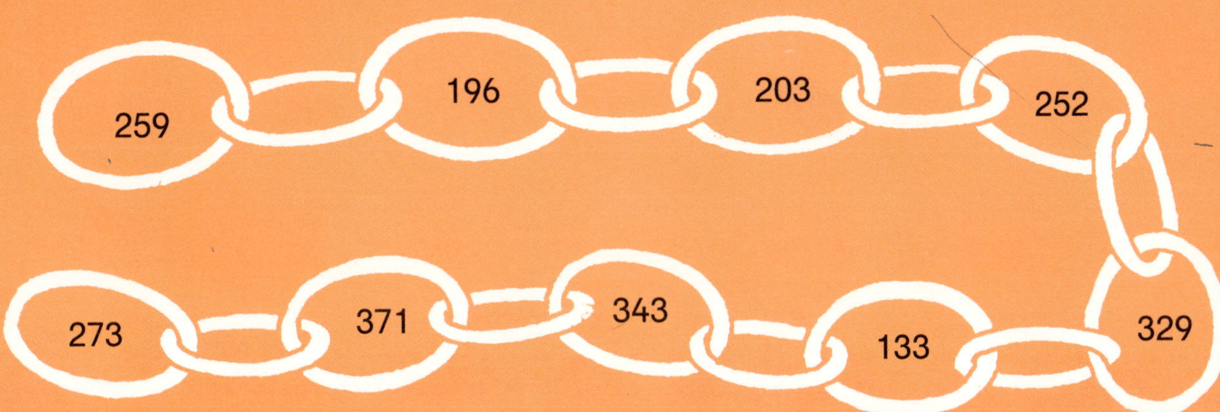

2. Which answers are **prime numbers**?

91 A **palindrome** reads the same backwards as forwards, for example 2662 or 9559.

Add or subtract a number less than 10 to make each of these a palindrome.

Write down each palindrome you make.

1. 1437	2. 2109	3. 4987	4. 1886
5. 2338	6. 1670	7. 1982	8. 2009
9. 2671	10. 1104	11. 9563	12. 1119

92 Write the factors for each of these numbers.

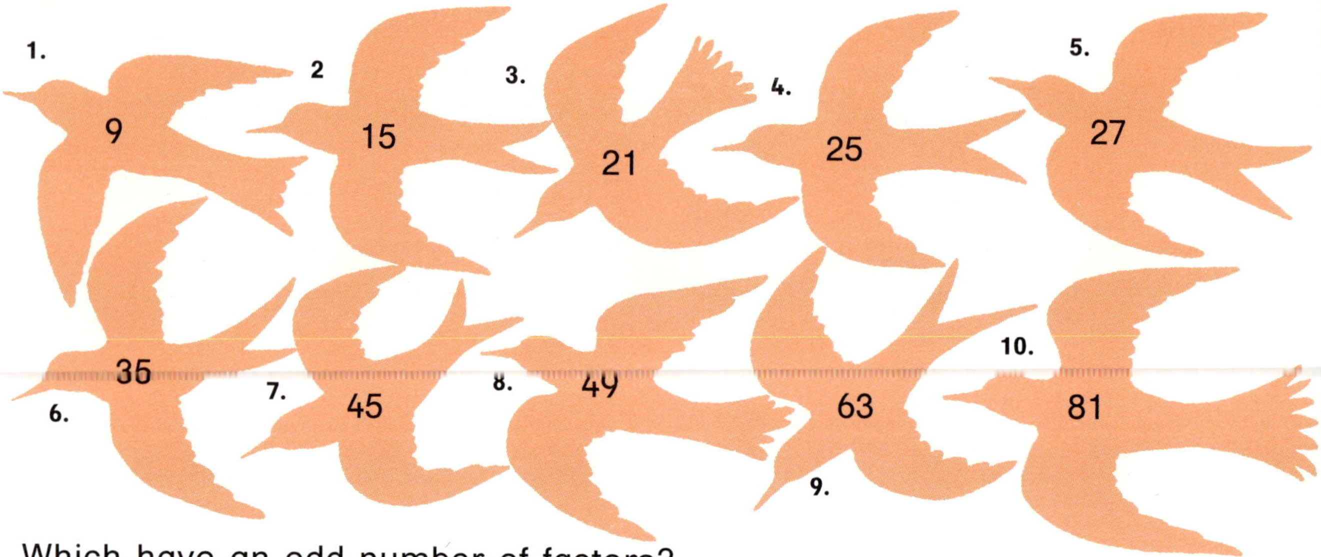

Which have an odd number of factors?
What is this set of numbers called?

93 Find the smallest number which has these factors.

1. 2, 5	2. 2, 3, 4, 6	3. 2, 4, 8
4. 2, 3, 6, 9	5. 2, 4, 5, 10	6. 2, 3, 4, 6, 8
7. 2, 4, 7	8. 2, 3, 5, 6, 10	9. 2, 3, 4, 6, 9
10. 2, 4, 5, 8, 10	11. 2, 3, 6, 7	12. 3, 5, 9

94 Each △ is a triangular number.

Each □ is a square number.

Find the missing numbers.

1. △ + □ = 51	2. □ − △ = 85
3. □ + △ = 30	4. △ − □ = 19
5. △ − □ = 2	6. □ + △ = 61
7. □ + △ = 35	8. □ − △ = 90
9. △ + □ = 40	10. △ + □ = 53

95 Use the digits in the order they are written.

Use + or − to make the smallest answer you can.

1. 1 ☐ 7 ☐ 4 ☐ 3 ☐ 2 =
2. 6 ☐ 5 ☐ 4 ☐ 8 ☐ 1 =
3. 5 ☐ 9 ☐ 3 ☐ 2 ☐ 8 =

Do the same again. Make the answer as near to 10 as you can.

4. 7 ☐ 5 ☐ 3 ☐ 2 ☐ 8 =
5. 9 ☐ 7 ☐ 6 ☐ 5 ☐ 4 =
6. 7 ☐ 2 ☐ 8 ☐ 4 ☐ 5 =

96 What has happened to each of these?

Rewrite them, putting in the missing numbers.

1. 4 $\xrightarrow{+\square\ \times\square}$ 15
2. 6 $\xrightarrow{\div\square\ +\square}$ 5
3. 10 $\xrightarrow{\div\square\ \times\square}$ 8
4. 6 $\xrightarrow{\times\square\ +\square}$ 20
5. 7 $\xrightarrow{-\square\ \times\square}$ 20
6. 20 $\xrightarrow{\div\square\ +\square}$ 8
7. 15 $\xrightarrow{\div\square\ \times\square}$ 9
8. 11 $\xrightarrow{-\square\ \div\square}$ 3

97 The table shows which letters the digits 0 to 9 stand for.

0	1	2	3	4	5	6	7	8	9
D	**E**	**H**	**S**	**T**	**R**	**A**	**O**	**N**	**U**

Add these pairs of numbers.

What word does each answer make?

1. 132 and 131
2. 199 and 279
3. 417 and 477
4. 428 and 140
5. 193 and 681
6. 159 and 201
7. 1843 and 2917
8. 1984 and 3776
9. 1959 and 6782

98 What never asks a question but is always answered?

Use the table to find the answer.

A	E	G	H	I	L	N	O	P	R	T
189	432	801	275	192	396	288	158	752	368	261

___	___	___	___	___	___	___	___
27 × 7	46 × 8	24 × 8	36 × 8	267 × 3	48 × 4	72 × 4	89 × 9

___	___	___	___	___	___	___	___	___
87 × 3	72 × 6	66 × 6	144 × 3	94 × 8	55 × 5	79 × 2	144 × 2	48 × 9

99 Look at the numbers which are opposite each other to complete each wheel.

1.

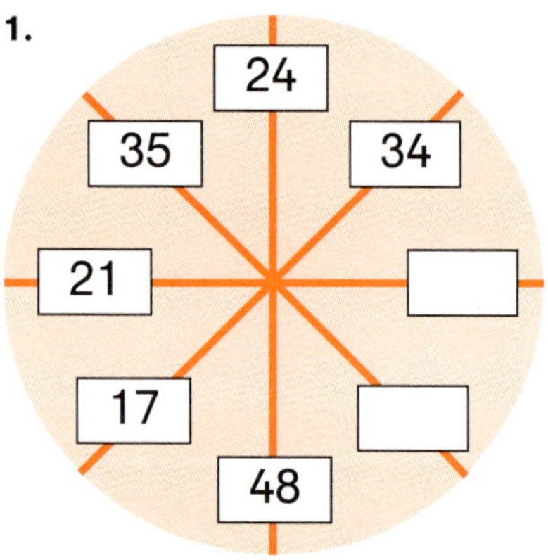

2.

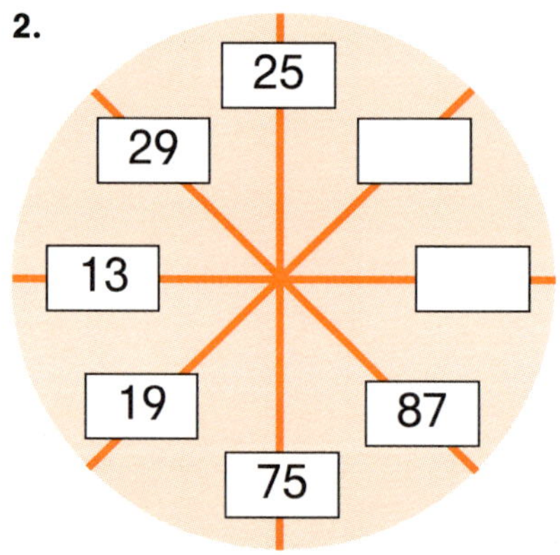

3.

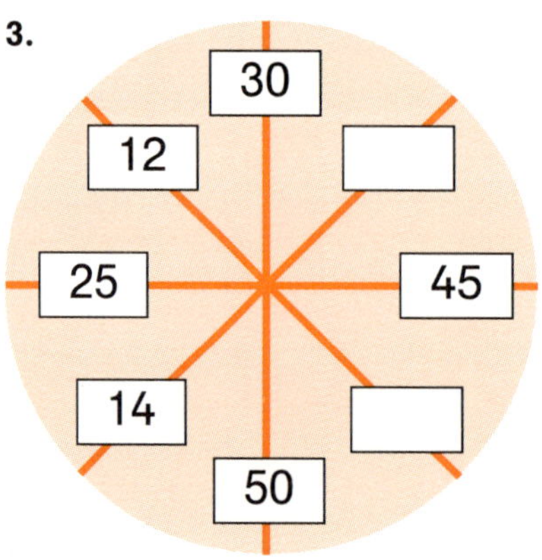

4.

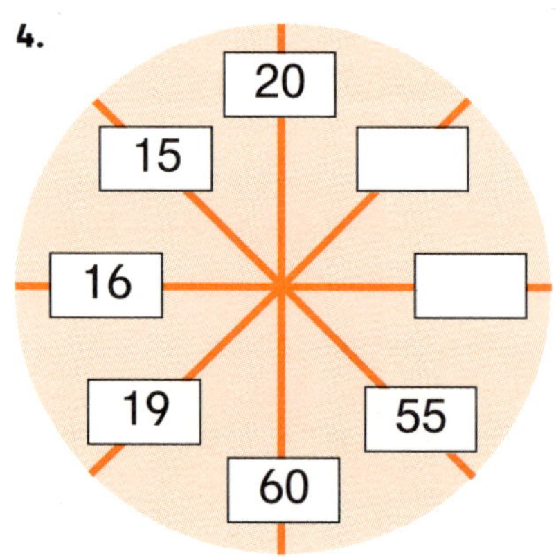

100

Use this table to solve the riddles.

A	B	E	G	I	K	L	N	P	R	T	W	Z
30	12	72	56	40	32	42	80	16	60	81	45	66

1. If you drop a white hat into the Black Sea, how does it come out?

Rearrange the letters for multiples of 9.

2. An old name for a Chinese city.

   Rearrange the letters for multiples of 8.

3. Name a coat that is always on fire.

   Rearrange the letters for multiples of 6.

101

Copy the grid but leave out two digits to make the total of each row and each column a multiple of 5.

3	4	1	7
2	6	1	2
4	5	9	1
1	6	8	5

102 Each pole is half as long as the one before.

Find the length of the shortest pole in each of these.

1.

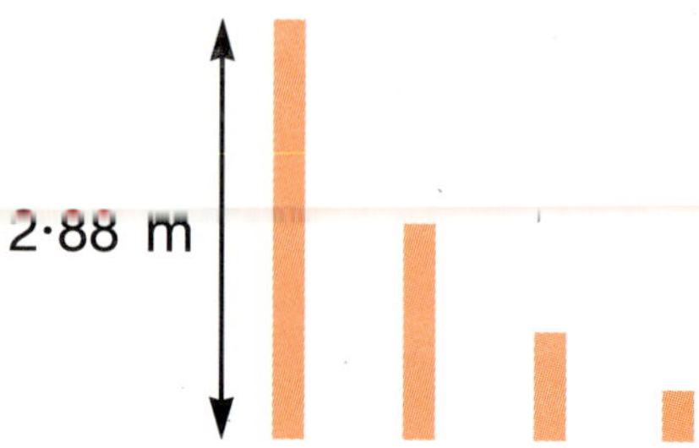

2.

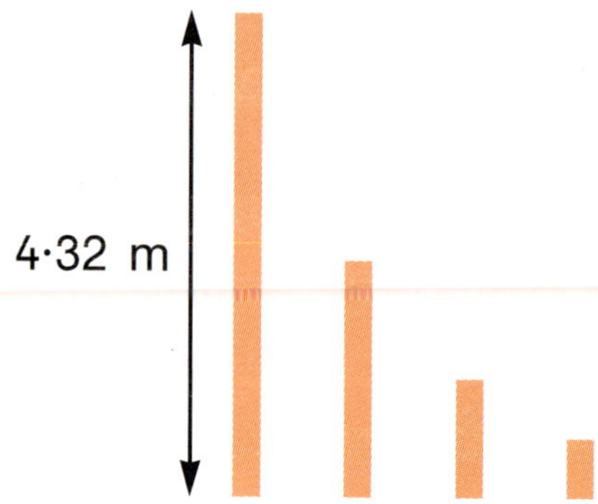

3.

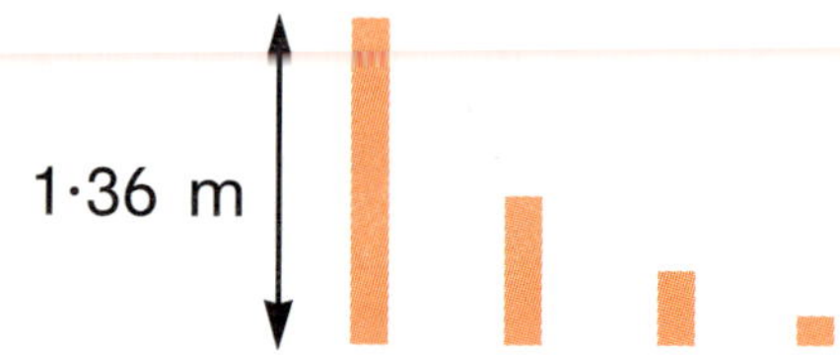

4.

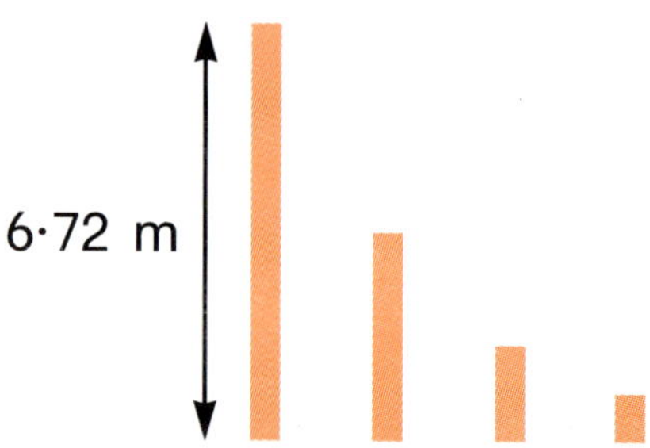

5.

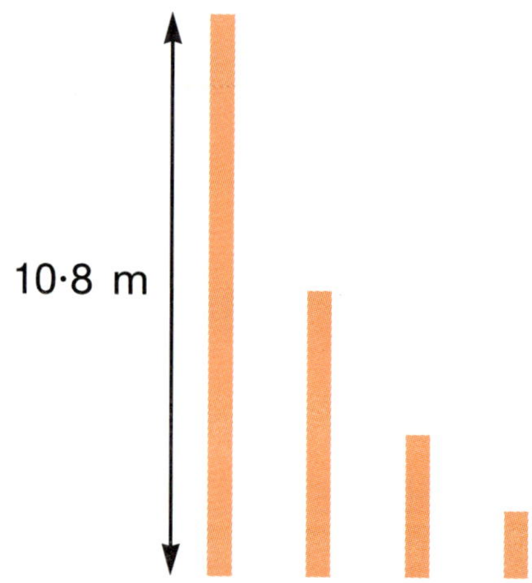

6.

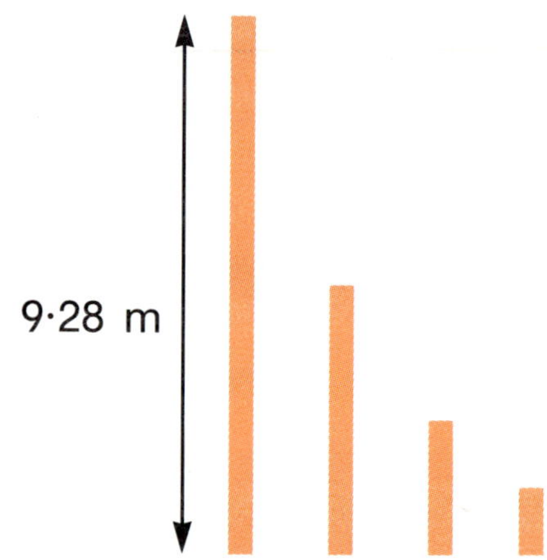

103 Match each label to a container.

A

B

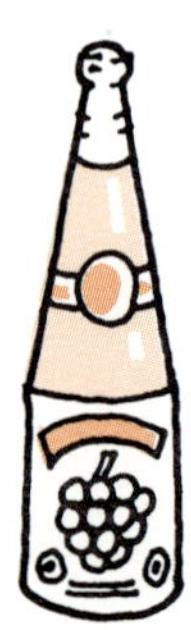

C

D

2 litres	4·5 litres	20 ml	700 ml

104 Who is nearest to the average height?

Alan	Brian	Carla	Denise
138 cm	134 cm	124 cm	136 cm

105 Who is nearest to the average weight?

Alan	Brian	Carla	Denise
49 kg	56 kg	47 kg	52 kg

106 What is the perimeter of each of these?

1.

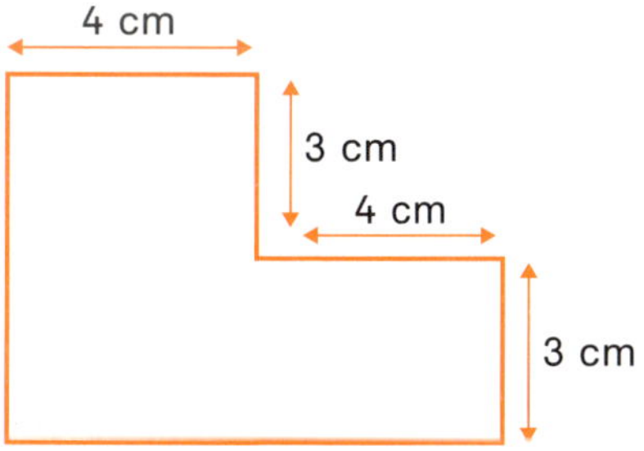

2.

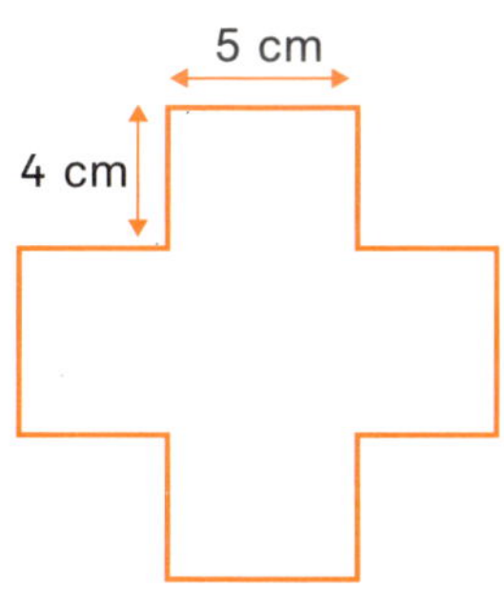

3.

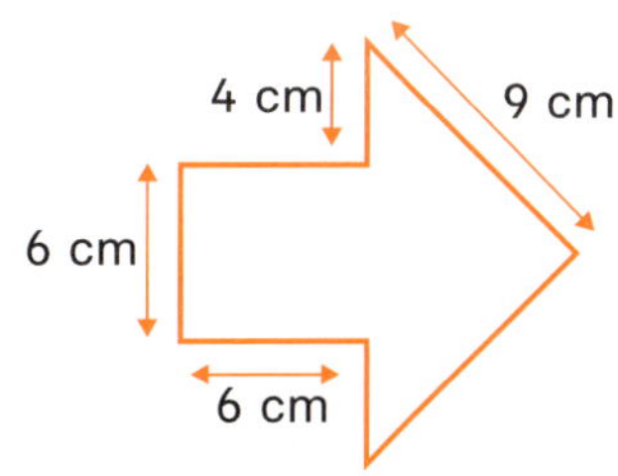

4.

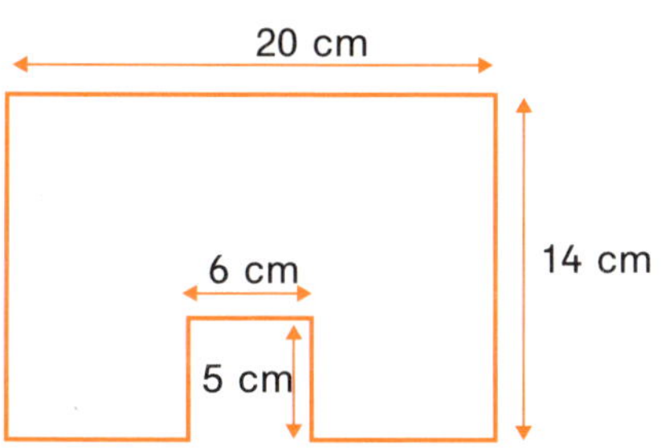

5.

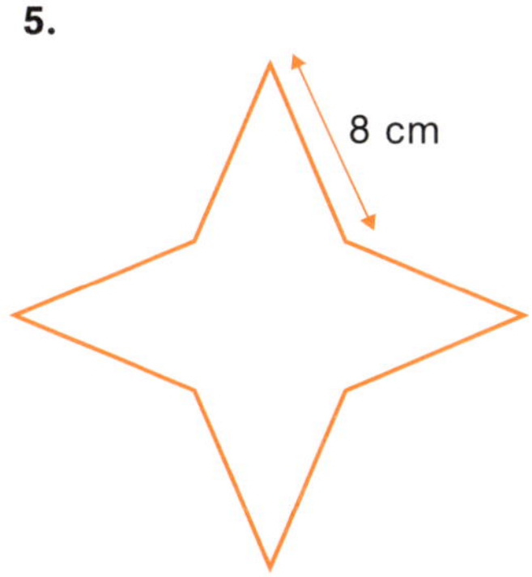

6.

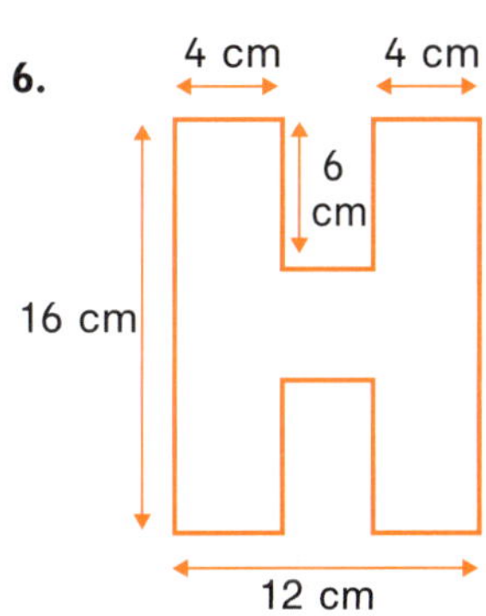

107

1. How many cm in $1\frac{1}{4}$ m?
2. How many g in $2\frac{1}{4}$ kg?
3. How many ml in $1\frac{3}{4}$ l?
4. How many seconds in 4 minutes?
5. How many minutes in $\frac{3}{4}$ hour?
6. How many metres in $2\frac{1}{2}$ km?
7. How many hours in 3 days?
8. How many mm in $2\frac{1}{2}$ cm?

108

1. It is −1 °C.
   The temperature rises by 4 °C.
   What is the new temperature?
2. It is 3:55 pm.
   What will the time be after 15 minutes?
3. How many minutes between 5:40 pm and 6:20 pm?
4. What is the cost of $2\frac{1}{2}$ metres at £4.50 per metre?
5. If 1 kg of nails costs 48p, what do $3\frac{1}{2}$ kg cost?
6. 4 metres of cloth cost £7.44.
   What does 1 metre cost?

109

1. How many 10 cm square tiles are needed to cover an area 1 m wide and 2 m long?
2. How many 1 cm cubes are needed to fill a box 5 cm long, 3 cm wide and 3 cm deep?

110 What must be added to make these measures up to the next whole unit?

1.	1·25 m	2.	3·120 kg	3.	2·350 l	4.	4·5 cm
5.	4·5 km	6.	1·5 l	7.	2·5 m	8.	3·5 kg
9.	$\frac{3}{4}$ m	10.	$1\frac{1}{4}$ kg	11.	$2\frac{1}{4}$ l	12.	$3\frac{3}{4}$ km

111 How many km will each travel in 2 hours?

1. A train  travels 3 km in a minute.

2. A car  travels 3 km in two minutes.

3. A cyclist  travels 500 m in three minutes.

4. A long distance runner  travels 750 m in five minutes.

112 Which is the heaviest?

A

B

C

113 What is the temperature?

1.

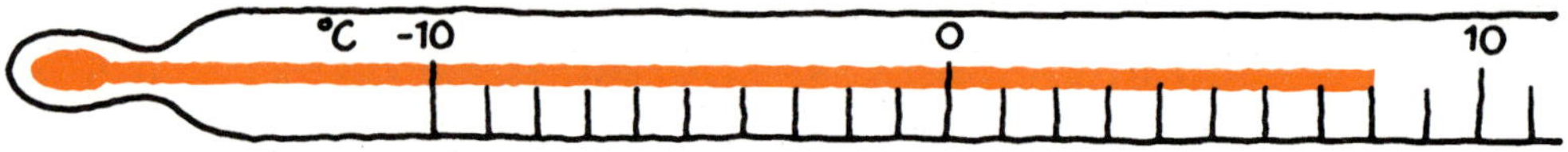

2.

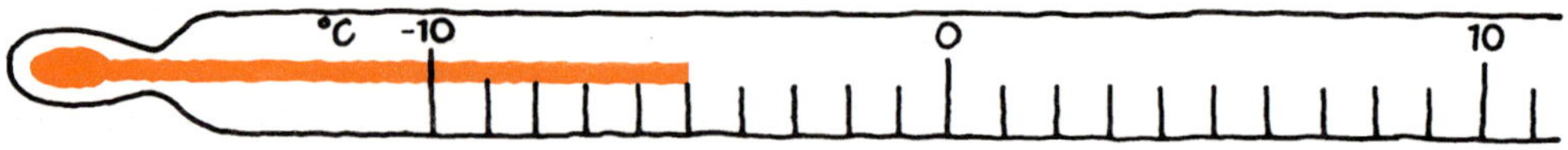

3.

4.

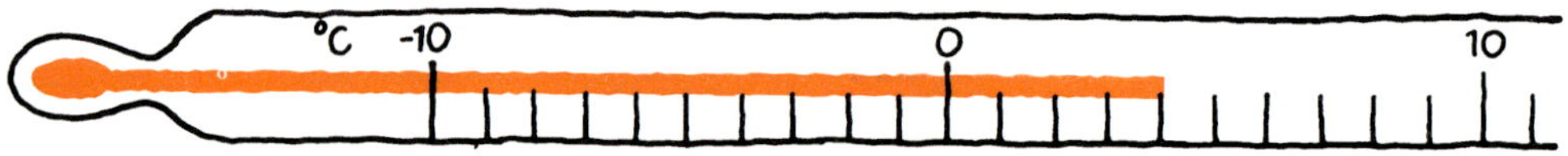

5.

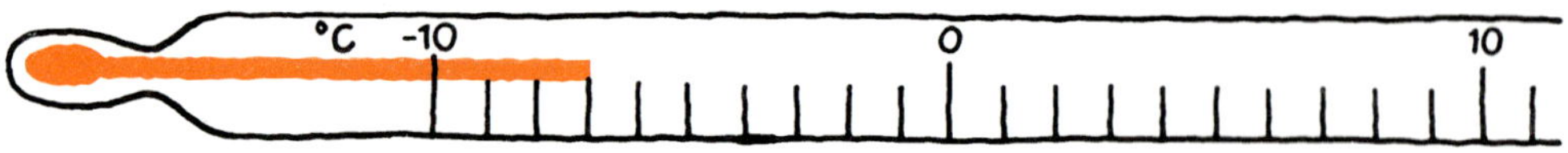

114 How many ml in each jar?

1. 2. 3. 4. 5.

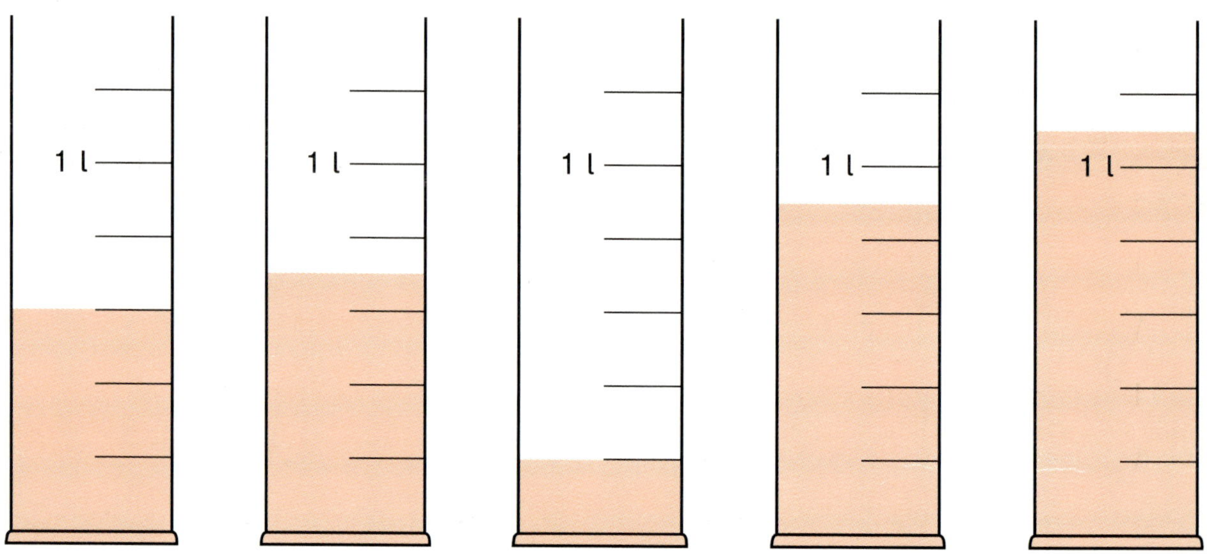

115

FARO (ALGARVE) **Date of outward journey and cost (return)**

FROM	Day	Outward Departure	Return Landing	01/11-16/11	17/11-23/11	24/11-10/12	11/12-17/12	18/12-24/12	26/12-31/12	01/01-28/01	29/01-11/02	12/02-25/02	26/02-04/03	05/03-08/04	09/04-13/04	14/04-20/04	21/04-29/04
Gatwick	Sun	0815	1410	**£104**	**£96**	**£79**	**£89**	**£159**	**£159**	**£89**	**£93**	**£109**	**£99**	**£104**	**£114**	**£159**	**£109**
Luton	Sun	0750	1400	**£108**	**£110**	**£83**	**£93**	**£163**	**£163**	**£93**	**£97**	**£113**	**£103**	**£108**	**£118**	**£163**	**£113**
Machester	Sun	0740	1405	**£121**	**£113**	**£96**	**£106**	**£176**	**£176**	**£106**	**£109**	**£129**	**£119**	**£124**	**£134**	**£176**	**£126**
Glasgow	Sun	1630	2355	**£139**	**£131**	–	–	**£194**	**£194**	**£129**	–	**£144**	**£134**	**£144**	**£194**	**£154**	**£149**

1. At what time does the Faro flight leave Glasgow?
2. At what time does the flight from Faro land at Luton?
3. Between which dates is the cheapest flight from Manchester?
4. What is the cost of a Gatwick to Faro return on 1st April?

116

CLIMATE: JAMAICA

Nov	Dec	Jan	Feb	Mar	Apr	May	Jun	Jul	Aug	Sep	Oct
31	30	29	29	31	32	32	33	33	33	33	32

Average daily maximum temperature °C

$8\frac{1}{2}$	$8\frac{1}{2}$	9	9	$9\frac{1}{2}$	10	9	9	10	$9\frac{1}{2}$	9	9

Average hours of sunshine per day

11	11	8	4	4	8	18	16	8	13	17	19

Average monthly rainfall in centimetres

83	83	83	83	81	80	83	80	79	80	81	83

Average monthly humidity %

CLIMATE: EGYPT (Cairo)

Nov	Dec	Jan	Feb	Mar	Apr	May	Jun	Jul	Aug	Sep	Oct
26	20	18	21	24	28	33	35	36	34	32	30

Average daily maximum temperature °C

9	8	7	8	10	11	11	12	12	12	11	10

Average hours of sunshine per day

–	1	1	1	1	–	–	–	–	–	–	–

Average monthly rainfall in centimetres

38	41	40	33	27	21	18	20	24	28	31	31

Average monthly humidity %

1. Which month, in Egypt, has the least sun?
2. Which is the hottest month in Egypt?
3. How many centimetres of rain fall in Jamaica in May on average?
4. What is the average maximum temperature in Egypt in August?
5. What are the daily average hours of sunshine in Jamaica in April?

117 This is a sorting tree.

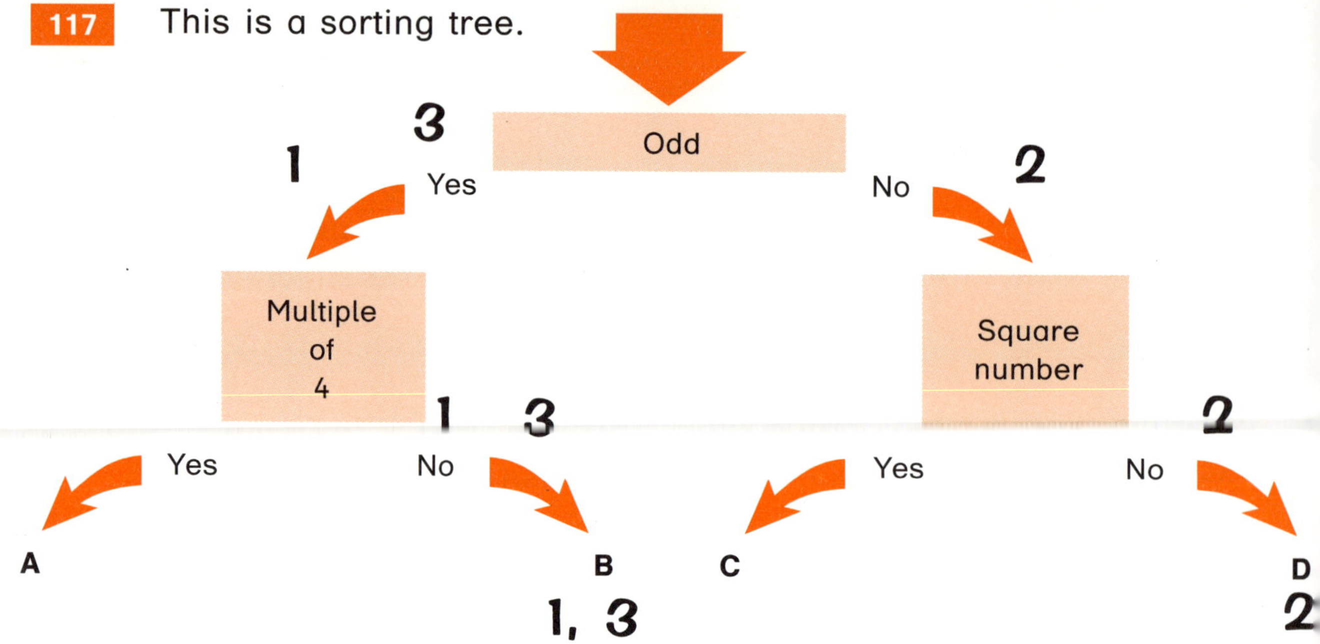

Sort the numbers to 20. Some have been done for you.

Which numbers come out at each letter?

118

Draw this diagram.
Write the numbers 1 to 20
in the regions.

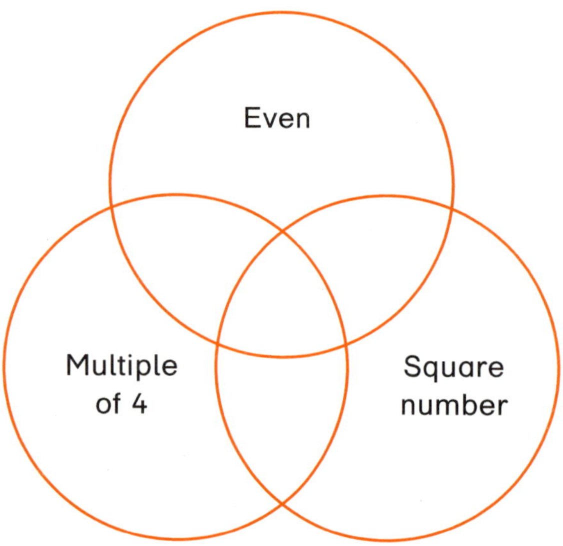

119

Draw this diagram.
Write the numbers 1 to 20
in the regions.

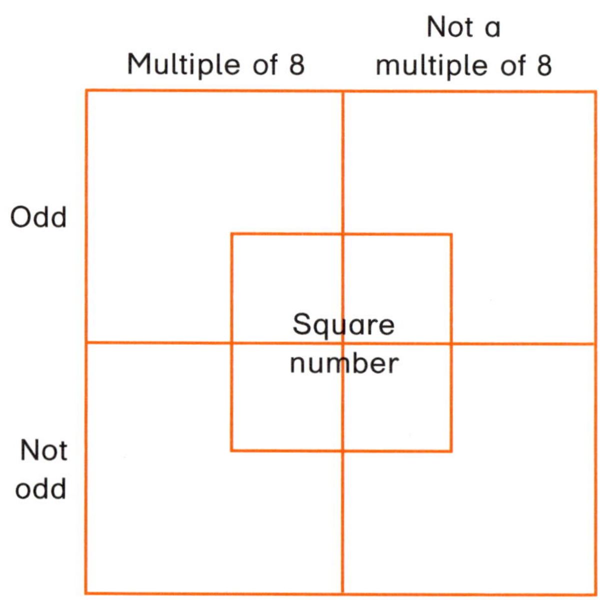